40 Seconds to Inner Peace

A Biblical Worldview & Credo

Steve D. Gardner

40 SECONDS TO INNER PEACE
A Biblical Worldview & Credo
Copyright © 2021 by Steve D. Gardner

All rights reserved. No portion of this book may be reproduced in any form without permission from the publisher, except as permitted by U.S. copyright law. For permissions contact: sgwriter49@gmail.com.

All Bible verses are identified.

NLT: New Living Translation, copyright © 1996, 2004, 2015 by Tyndale House Foundation. Used by permission of Tyndale House Publishers, Inc., Carol Stream, Illinois 60188. All rights reserved.

ESV: English Standard Version. ESV® Text Edition: 2016. Copyright © 2001 by Crossway Bibles, a publishing ministry of Good News Pub.

NIV: New International Version®, NIV® Copyright ©1973, 1978, 1984, 2011 by Biblica, Inc.® Used by permission. All rights reserved.

NASB: New American Standard Bible®, Copyright © 1960, 1971, 1977, 1995, 2020 by The Lockman Foundation. All rights reserved.

AMP: Amplified Bible (AMP) Copyright © 2015 by The Lockman Foundation, La Habra, CA 90631. All rights reserved.

TLB: The Living Bible copyright © 1971 by Tyndale House Foundation. Used by permission of Tyndale House Publishers Inc., Carol Stream, Illinois 60188. All rights reserved.

CEV: Contemporary English Version (CEV) Copyright © 1995 by American Bible Society

MSG: The Message (MSG) Copyright © 1993, 2002, 2018 by Eugene H. Peterson

GNT: Good News Translation (GNT) Copyright © 1992 by American Bible Society

NCV: New Century Version®. Copyright © 2005 by Thomas Nelson, Inc.

GW: GOD'S WORD Translation. Copyright © 1995, 2003, 2013, 2014, 2019, 2020 by God's Word to the Nations Mission Society. All rights reserved.

MEV: Modern English Version. Copyright © 2014 by Military Bible Association. Published and distributed by Charisma House.

PHILLIPS: The New Testament in Modern English by J.B Phillips copyright © 1960, 1972 J. B. Phillips. Administered by The Archbishops' Council of the Church of England. Used by Permission.

TPT: The Passion Translation®. Copyright © 2017, 2018, 2020 by Passion & Fire Ministries, Inc. Used by permission. All rights reserved. thePassionTranslation.com

Cover Design: Steve D. Gardner with technical assistance from Kingof_Designer

Cover Photos: Front: Jordan Steranka on Unsplash

Back: Tony Lee on Unsplash

ISBN: 978-1-7369261-2-3

Acknowledgements

I owe a thank you to everyone I've ever known, even the bad examples from whom I've learned lessons.

But mostly I recall the good examples, like praying grandparents whose spiritual warfare on my behalf will not be fully revealed until heaven.

My parents, in their nineties as of this writing, provided a nurturing home in which the desire to follow Jesus was the norm.

My wife, Maria, is the love of my life. As my primary support, collaborator, sounding board, and encourager, she has been indispensable. We aspire to reach our 75th anniversary one of these days. Why not? We're past our 53rd at this point and don't feel much different than we did in college.

Several friends have done me the honor of being beta readers and making suggestions that have strengthened this message. Thank you, Dave and Syd Phelps, Ed and Kay Halderman, the Brett and Mandy Fish family, Dr. Bob Nienhuis, Brad Gardner, and Daryle Doden. I am deeply grateful for your input.

Contents

Acknowledgements vi
1 Awaking Awareness 1
2 Problems 7
3 In Your Best Interest 11
4 Why This Is So Worth Your Time 17
5 Making Connections 23
6 Meet the Peace Credo 31
7 God's Identity – the Foundation for Everything 37
8 God's Identity – Creator 43
9 God's Identity – Sovereign 51
10 God's Identity – Providential 59
11 God's Identity – Redemptive 65
12 My Identity – Loved 73
13 My Identity – Child 81
14 My Identity – Redeemed 87
15 My Identity – Being transformed daily 93
16 Choosing to Trust 99
17 Trusting God's Plan 105
18 Understanding 111
19 Trust Before Understanding 119

20 Gratitude	127
21 God's Good Plan	135
22 God Working out His Good Plan in My Life	141
23 When the Plan Doesn't Seem So Good	147
24 The Positive Response of Repentance	155
25 The Boogeyman	163
26 Living Fully Forgiven – Passport to Freedom	169
27 Getting People off Your Hook	175
28 Letting Go of the Hook	181
29 The Final Line	191

1

Awaking Awareness

Sitting in Denver's Gate C32 waiting for my flight to Orlando, I hear our gate agent announce a delay over the intercom. Good thing I have a book along. But I might not get to it in this day full of distractions.

The fortyish man sitting across from me appears to have little in common with the thirtyish woman two seats away. He is tall, well built, and ruggedly handsome. She is on the short side, not exactly petite, and average in appearance.

His mussed hair and $2000 vagabond outfit (including designer sunglasses) seems to say he cares a lot about looking like he doesn't care. She's wearing an attractive, comfortable dress she might have gotten on sale at Nordstrom Rack for $40.

But that is only the beginning of the differences. Talking intensely on his phone, he is in and out of his seat, pacing the nearby floorspace and occasionally edging a bit farther away when he raises his voice in a tirade of curses at his employee.

The woman, on the other hand, patiently tries to settle a dispute with an insurance company after the passing of her mother. What these two have most in common is having to deal with bad news in a difficult situation. What they have least in common is how they deal with it.

What makes the difference? What enables peace for one person in circumstances that cause a major eruption in another? I have no idea what their specific situations are, and I'm not about to judge them. They just happen in this moment to illustrate a noticeable contrast. It makes me want to know more.

The gate attendant just now updates the status of my flight. Another delay. I can't believe they're doing this to me. Especially today. Do they have any idea how important my meeting is? A churning knot in my gut is a clue that stress is having a physically destructive impact.

I hear a voice behind me. "Are you breaking up with me?" The intensity grows. "Is that what this is?"

Surprised at how public this private conversation seems to be, I turn to get a closer look. A couple, probably in their late twenties, is walking toward the end of the concourse. I don't know if they're on their way to a convention, the in-laws, or their honeymoon, but they are totally absorbed in their own world and oblivious to everyone around them.

"Maybe it is," he says. "Is that what you want?"

"You jerk!" she yells in a voice that must have found listeners two gates away. "How dare you pull this now! Are you deliberately trying to ruin my life?"

"Calm down," he says and then mumbles something as they pass beyond my hearing.

I think about following them to get the rest of the story, but then think better of it. I've got my own problems, including this flight delay. It dawns on me that the "they" who are causing my flight delay – the people doing this to me – are probably no happier about it than I am. And they are certainly not "doing this *to me.*"

The realization helps my attitude with the gate attendant, but it doesn't solve my problem. And my problem is on two levels: first, the fallout because of the meeting I am likely to miss, and second, just as important, how my perspective will shape that fallout.

I've learned a lot since that day, and I continue to explore the implications as I apply new insights.

You and I are about to examine together how we see life, how we process what happens to us, and most importantly, how we build the habits that give us inner peace.

Born out of need
Some life-changing choices begin in stealth mode.

This one crept up on me five years ago. It dawned on me that my occasional awareness of God's presence in my life was lame. So was my degree of trust in him.

I needed to radically improve in my awareness that he is with me 24/7 and that I could and should trust him implicitly.

My natural tendency is to second guess him, assuming I have to understand and approve what he's doing in my life before I can get fully onboard. That's worse than lame: it's crippling.

I decided to devote the next period of my life – however long it would take – to focus on awareness and trust until they became second nature.

This book has grown out of those choices as I have wrestled with how to overcome my natural liabilities.

I don't pretend to have arrived. I still experience moments of concern (my "spiritual" word for worry), moments of frustration (anger), and moments of distrust (stupid arrogance). But they don't last as long.

Now, most of the time they are just moments, as my new habits of awareness and attitude see them for what they are and replace them with much healthier perspectives.

Bold promises

I make quite a few promises in this book, because for me it's no longer theory. Instead, this is how God is actively renewing my mind in the process of transforming me into his image bearer, day by day, moment by moment.

Taking forty seconds to recite my personal credo – a biblical worldview in shorthand – isn't a huge investment of time or energy. But as a maintenance call after learning the depth of its foundational truths, it is powerful.

Once you have taken the time to read this book and unpack the Scriptures behind the Peace Credo, you too may find those forty seconds to be rich with insights that flash through your head and heart. God's word is alive, and his peace comes home.

As time goes on, the work of seeing life from a better perspective becomes easier. And richer. And more automatic as new habits of thinking replace the old ones. Peace gives birth to happiness that has staying power – a deep joy that the world cannot understand and cannot ever take away. I want this for you.

God's plan for us is unfolding moment by moment. We shouldn't expect to fully understand it – any more than we could understand living in a dozen dimensions when we can only sense four. But we can choose to trust him and his plan.

And it amazes me how choosing to trust God before understanding what he's up to hastens my journey to understanding.

2

Problems

Let's bring it home to you. Your problems, although vexing in the moment, may be on the mundane side: trying to pay the bills without adding to your credit card debt; strategizing how to parent a strong-willed toddler with unlimited energy (or harder yet – a teenager); balancing the work/family tug of war where you feel like no one wins.

Or maybe you're in the middle of your worst nightmare.

- You lose your job.
- You fail a crucial exam.
- You lose the person you love most in the world.
- Your identity is stolen, resulting in huge losses you may not be able to recover.
- You are falsely accused of a horrible crime that could cost your reputation and freedom.
- You cause an accident that severely injures others.
- A stock market crash suddenly slashes your net worth in half.
- You are diagnosed with a life-threatening disease.

Will you panic? Will you passively retreat and hope the problem vanishes? Will you lash out recklessly at the injustice?

Clearly, panic is not the answer. Isaiah reassures that you're not alone. *"Don't panic. I'm with you.*

There's no need to fear for I'm your God. I'll give you strength. I'll help you. I'll hold you steady, keep a firm grip on you" (Isaiah 41:10, MSG).

Neither is passivity the answer. But peace is not passive, and it is the first thing you need to become a victor rather than a victim. Do you know how to get it before you have final resolution of the problem? That's the purpose of this book.

No problems?
We can also approach this subject from the opposite direction. Set aside the grim scenarios. No matter what your current status – employed or not, married or not, healthy or not, rich or not – you want to be consistently happy. Essential to that kind of contentment is a quality that quietly undergirds it: the quality of peace.

If we lack inner peace, we can't experience happiness beyond momentary pleasures that depend on external circumstances and evaporate as quickly as they appear.

Sometimes we are aware of a lack of peace, but most of the time it hides behind other symptoms. What we feel is a low-grade, general unhappiness. Upon closer inspection, we might describe it as a combination of unfulfillment, loss of direction, unclear purpose, and little joy. In more advanced stages, it progresses to anger, bitterness, and cynicism.

Inner peace, on the other hand, can thrive in the middle of a war that threatens our life. My goal is to unveil a process that leads to an inner peace that transcends the storms we all encounter.

Internal angst

Do you have an internal angst that longs to be quieted, to be at peace? How do you get that peace? Certainly not from entertainment or whatever its endless ads are promoting.

Simply increasing the flow of information is not the answer; we're overloaded with digital input. Some of it is helpful, but much of it is counter-productive to our wellbeing – especially in large doses.

Our increasingly biased news sources have become little more than hucksters for social and political agendas. Even the least-biased news sources contribute more to personal anxiety than to peace. Endless images of global problems far beyond our personal sphere of influence create an angst we cannot resolve. Our brain triggers its normal fight or flight response, but with no immediate threat to respond to, we suffer a generalized anxiety that drains our adrenal system. Ever wonder where your energy has gone?

The numbing effects of alcohol and drugs, the thrill of gambling, the comfort of overeating and "shopping therapy" are all momentary escapes that end up compounding our troubles.

With no personal solutions in sight, anxiety increases. We want desperately to make sense of it all, to bring meaning to it, but it's an uphill battle. We interpret each day's events based on assumptions our mind has accepted as valid – even though many of them remain unchallenged by the light of God's truth.

Truth to the rescue
Since Satan, *"the father of lies,"* takes advantage of our vulnerability by twisting every truth into a convincing counterfeit, he stokes our natural fears and robs us of the peace that should be ours as a child of God.

But truth is not so easily disposed of. It exists independently of perception and interpretation. It endures regardless of what you or I think about it. When ignorance, misunderstandings, confusion, and deceptions die away, the truth will still be standing. It will be seen for what it is, and it will reveal us for what we are, both good and bad.

Because none of us can claim to meet God's righteous standard on our own, his redemptive truth is our only defense against judgment.

We need to make friends with the truth now. In fact, one of the wisest promises we can make to ourselves is to strive throughout life to make all truth our best friend – whether it's convenient or not, whether it puts us in the best light or not, whether it's comfortable or not.

Truth cannot be broken, but we can break ourselves against it like a ship on the rocks after failing to align with the harbor channel. The Peace Credo is all about aligning ourselves with enduring truth.

3

In Your Best Interest

Can you remember a moment when all the pieces came together and you felt the joy of being in complete harmony with God and the world? If yes, to what do you attribute it? If you're not there at this moment, what do you think has changed? What was different then?

If you've never had such a moment, would you like to experience one? And make it frequent? What gets in the way? What makes you react in ways that undermine inner peace rather than foster it?

Unfortunately, you have a problem. I know this because I have the same one. It's universal: *We are driven to actions that are often not in our best interest.*

Two simple questions

Take a moment to consider two simple questions. These will help you identify your unique version of the universal problem we share. I say your unique version because we all differ in terms of aptitudes, abilities, dreams, vulnerabilities, fears, etc. We're alike in that we all have them, but each of us has our unique constellation. Note the first thoughts that come to your head.

1. What do you dream about, wishing it could happen?
2. What do you worry about? What is behind the occasional dull ache in the pit of your stomach?

Desire and fear are powerful motivators of action. Desire is what we wish for; fear is what we wish to avoid. Both are more emotional than rational, but we act in accordance with them, even when we haven't identified them precisely.

Sometimes we convince ourselves that a surface reason for an action is the whole story, but it rarely is. Underlying desires and fears are the hidden motivators that both drive us and conflict us as they battle in the shadows.

For example, why did good old John send a check to his relative who asked for yet another loan in a string of broken promises to repay? Is it simply because they "needed" it? Or were there deeper desires like John's need to be appreciated and seen as the rescuer? Or deeper fears like being perceived as selfish and uncaring?

I raise the questions simply to reveal the conflicting desires and fears that work in our subconscious, driving us to actions that are not in our best interest. You know it happens. Your life history is filled with incidents that prove it. Incidents you regret and later ask yourself, "What was I thinking?" Or more often, "What was I NOT thinking?"

What kind of defective autopilot causes these incidents? More importantly, how do we fix it? These next two sentences are crucial.

1. You do not need to psychoanalyze yourself to transform your life.
2. You can gain awareness and routine realignment with truth that leads to inner peace even before you understand how it all works.

In your best interest

When I suggest that you are driven to actions that are often not in your best interest, you might ask, What about everyone else's best interest? If you're concerned that "in your best interest" could lead to selfish rationalization, let me congratulate you. Such a sensitivity is well placed.

However, when the phrase "in your best interest" occurs in this book, it does not refer to something selfish, as in a grab for limited resources. Instead, it means your long-term best interest (think eternal), your best interest from God's point of view as well as yours when you are wise enough to agree with God. *"He who loves wisdom loves his **own best interest** and will be a success"* (Proverbs 19:8, TLB, emphasis added).

Your long-term best interest clearly rules out immediate self-gratification that is inevitably bundled with delayed consequences. Smoking, substance abuse, and overeating are easy examples of this category. So are illicit sex, overspending, and gossip.

Your long-term best interest also rules out actions that, if discovered, would harm your reputation. Examples include lying, cheating, stealing, and law breaking in general. Even more important than your reputation is your true character, and such actions undermine it even if you manage to hide the truth from family and friends for a long time.

Think of it this way: anything God prohibits is not in your best interest. Anything you want – while wrestling with a nagging feeling that God would disapprove – is not in your best interest. If you can think of an exception, one of two things must be true:

- you misunderstand God's identity and character, or
- you misunderstand the thing you want; you don't have enough foresight to realize how it will cheat you in the end.

Another way to say it: Make sure you want what your wants lead to. Many appealing doors open to dark rooms leading to ever-deepening regret. You might want what an attractive door promises, but you may despise what lies behind it.

To summarize: Anything within God's will for you is in your best interest. The converse is also true: Anything in your best interest is within God's will for you.

So, what is my solution to the age-old dilemma of aligning my actions to God's will? The Bible gives us all the necessary truths we need. The missing link is how to engage with them in a way that transforms our natural patterns of thinking.

What is a credo?
Webster defines credo as "a guiding belief or principle," adding that it "comes straight from the Latin word meaning 'I believe,' and is the first word of many religious creeds, such as the Apostles' Creed and the Nicene Creed."

In some ways it is like a creed, but it isn't as comprehensive. Instead, it is usually more focused on a specific topic or purpose.

The value of a credo

Most of us have used songs, poems, and memory devices of one kind or another to help us recall important information. We memorize Bible verses because we know God's word is supernatural and transformative. Many people memorize prayers to raise awareness, focus attention, refine perspective, and adjust attitude.

Taking my cue from these ideas, I wanted to combine them, add one more element, and make inner peace the focus. The additional element is the logical organization of foundational biblical truths into a concise credo that I can groove deeply into my head and heart.

It's an abbreviated worldview that, like poetry, implies content far beyond its few words. This makes it easy to repeat from memory for frequent awareness, not repetitiously, but at least daily. It's not a chant or a rant; it is a prayer combining scriptural truth with a confession of obedience.

I realize that evangelicals generally shy away from memorizing anything other than Scripture, and I understand why. We have a reasonable fear of what could become mindless repetition, or even worse, a religious good luck charm. However, the same could be said of repeating the Lord's Prayer or the twenty-third Psalm. You can mindlessly race through them without benefit or thoughtfully pray them for great benefit.

Why a credo?

Consider this simple analogy from Henry David Thoreau. "As a single footstep will not make a path on the earth, so a single thought will not make a pathway on the mind. To make a deep physical path, we walk again and again. To make a deep mental path, we must think over and over the kind of thoughts we wish to dominate our lives."

The rest of this book unveils the 40-second Peace Credo, a prayer that incorporates a biblical worldview in seven lines, only 75 words. Because our worldview is the lens through which we evaluate everything and make every decision, I can't overstate how important this is.

If I asked you to describe your worldview, you might not know where to start or what it includes. If so, you would be in the majority, but that doesn't mean you don't have a worldview. You do. Everyone does. And your worldview drives your decisions just as surely as the moon's gravity, although hidden, drives the tides.

The Peace Credo will help you create new habits of thought for interpreting your identity, the events in your life, and how God is using them to accomplish his good plan for you. This brings a resilient inner peace, enabling you to feel the joy of being in harmony with God and the world.

We'll unpack the credo together, exploring its alignment with underlying Scriptures that daily calibrate your identity, attitudes, and priorities.

Think of it as transitioning from a focus on the pain of problems to the joy of Inner Peace. *"Now may the Lord of peace himself give you **his peace** at all times and in every situation"* (2 Thessalonians 3:16, NLT, emphasis added).

4

Why This Is So Worth Your Time

This chapter is especially for cautious decision makers (or skeptics) who need a little more evidence to recognize the value of a well-crafted credo.

Would you like peace and joy to occupy the driver's seat in your life most of the time? What choice below best fits your style for trying to make it happen?

A. Not thinking about it; just letting nature take its course
B. Wishing for it; praying for it
C. Working hard to get ahead so my savings and investments will provide for the unexpected
D. Striving to anticipate and control future events; creating a detailed life plan
E. Daily aligning my worldview and attitudes with God's revealed truth

All of these have their proponents. The question is whether "A" through "D" really deliver or whether they keep the promised land of inner peace just out of reach.

"E" attacks the root of the issue, our basic perspective that constantly drifts out of proper alignment with God's revealed truth. The only way to combat this drift is the continuous renewing of our mind by the truth of God's word. A succinct, logical sequence enables us to focus on building trust that leads to inner peace.

How your brain works

The next two sections of this chapter deal with your worldview and your intuition. Before I get into the weeds on these, let me oversimplify how your brain works.

Your brain stores and interacts with an endless supply of facts, feelings, assumptions, and beliefs. These bits and pieces translate into action through three distinct processes. (1) Intuition: your brain subconsciously processes at blinding speed, and it does this virtually all the time. (2) Conscious analysis: during your waking hours, your brain analyzes any considerations it deems important.

Both of these processes – intuition and conscious analysis – lead to conclusions and behavior. They also lead to the third distinct action process. (3) Habits: these include habits of perspective and attitude, and they can be good or bad as they drive your behaviors. You want good habits, obviously, and you need a reliable path to helpful ones that bring inner peace and positive productivity.

Your worldview

We all have a worldview. Some of the most important components of your worldview include basic questions like, Who am I? Where did I come from? Why am I here? How can I find lasting fulfillment?

Any serious attempt to answer these questions forces you to examine what you believe about origins, origins of the universe, life in general, and your life specifically. If there is a designer/creator, what is his nature? What authority does he have? Am I under any obligation to him? Is it possible for me to relate to him in some way? If so, is he trustworthy? Are there consequences if I ignore him?

Your answers to these kinds of questions form your worldview. Whether crude or refined through years of consideration, they are the foundation for the direction of your life.

If you're like most people, they rarely rise to the surface of your consciousness – partly because they are so big and metaphysical that they defy simple proof. The seemingly endless follow-up questions tempt you to stuff them back into your brain's attic to wait for a more convenient time.

Unfortunately, your pace of life prevents a more convenient time from coming. So these and other all-important questions and their partially formed answers stay in the attic in a sort of stasis – present but not consciously active.

Your intuition

Meanwhile, an invisible autopilot – your intuition – operates unnoticed in the background, driving most of your behavior. You may object that you are not the intuitive type or that you consciously resist giving in to intuition because you prefer the safety of logical analysis.

Most people strive to analyze logically when making conscious decisions that have significant consequences, but these are a tiny fraction of the thousands of lesser decisions you make every day.

Yet even these lesser decisions rise in importance as they shuffle into your memory banks, creating new pathways and interconnections. This underscores the need to acknowledge and understand the role of intuition in daily life. It also relates to why the Peace Credo is so valuable.

Webster defines intuition as "the power or faculty of attaining direct knowledge or cognition without evident rational thought and inference." A key word is "evident," because rational thought and inference underlie intuition even though they are not evident in the moment.

Intuition is much more than an illogical conclusion or a mere guess. Instead, it is logic on steroids – seemingly instant conclusions that release us to act quickly.

Your brain is remarkable. The majority of its processing occurs without your conscious involvement or even your awareness. In fact, a third of it happens during sleep, because most of your brain remains active while the rest of your body sleeps.

But even the thoughts that dominate your consciousness during your waking hours are dwarfed by the subconscious decisions your brain's autopilot constantly processes. How many times have you thought, I'll clear my throat now, or, I'll wiggle my foot while I'm reading this, or, I'll cough now? You don't consciously think it; you just do it.

However, your brain will push the cough thought into your consciousness if you are in public and want to protect others from the virus it could project into the room.

But first it subconsciously processes many assumptions: (a) a physical discomfort has arisen in your chest or throat, (b) coughing can provide temporary relief; (c) you may have a contagious condition; (d) your cough could infect someone else; (e) others may be fearful even if you have no contagious condition; (f) you could cover your mouth with your hand, but (g) your hand touches other people, objects, and surfaces – all of which could transmit a virus. Finally, you consciously choose to cough into your arm at the elbow.

You make this one conscious decision on the heels of many thoughts your brain processed before you had time to consciously think through them. And even the thought to cough into your arm may have been subconscious if it has become your habit of choice.

How does your brain do all of this? It relies on prior processing. All the assumptions two paragraphs ago were consciously processed at some earlier point in your life.

When you accepted each of them as valid conclusions, your brain made logical connections between them and created an auto-response so you wouldn't have to take the time to consciously evaluate each one all over again. The urge to cough triggered an automatic action.

Your brain is constantly assembling assumptions into logical clusters for quick response. Over time, it assembles these clusters into super clusters of beliefs, enabling you to make what seem like giant leaps from a stimulus to an action you believe to be appropriate, all without conscious rational analysis in the moment.

This is just one example of how intuition works as a constant behavioral autopilot. Since it relies on previously processed assumption clusters and beliefs – some reliable and some not – you are wise to build the habit of aligning them with truth. The Peace Credo does this.

5

Making Connections

Connection between intuition and worldview
Why is it important to understand all of this? Because not all of your assumptions are as valid as the ones in the cough illustration. Whether in childhood or later in life, your brain has accepted many flawed assumptions as being valid.

These flawed assumptions are embedded with other assumptions, creating the clusters and super clusters that fuel your intuition. Some of these super clusters are at work in the foundation of your worldview, affecting what you see, how you interpret it, and how you react to it – all with blinding speed.

Your intuition is always active, melding assumptions, beliefs, emotions, and sensory inputs into the thousands of daily decisions that define your existence.

This is why the discipline of critical thinking is important. Its goal is to improve the quality of your decisions by analyzing *how* you think and improving it by adding some quality controls.

Summary statement: Your current assumption clusters fuel the autopilot of your intuition, which drives most of your behavior. If this summary statement doesn't rattle your cage, please reread it. *Your current assumption clusters fuel the autopilot of your intuition, which drives most of your behavior.*

Not understanding this is like not understanding that gasoline fuels the engine that powers your car. Defective gasoline will foul the engine and ruin your car's performance. Flawed assumptions will mislead your intuition and ruin the quality of your decisions.

As a result, you need two things: first, refined beliefs that increasingly align with enduring truth (reality); and second, a way to get these beliefs from your head to your heart, where your intuition can act on them quickly and consistently.

The Peace Credo supports both of these, helping you consistently recognize and replace actions that are not in your best interest.

Your best interest and your health

If the preceding doesn't seem urgent enough to motivate you, please pause to realize that actions not in your best interest lead inevitably to health problems in four dimensions.

1. Physical health

I don't need to tell you that a whole host of behaviors are proven to result in your body's inability to function at a high level. Alcohol and drug abuse are obvious threats to health, and yet people develop these addictions in spite of knowing better. Why?

There is an immediate payoff, excitement that masquerades as happiness, comfort, or peace. But the payoff dissipates quickly as the delayed consequences kick in and cause long-term pain. Overeating, poor nutrition, lack of exercise — all of these have a momentary sense of pleasure or peace — but the moment passes.

The expectation of repeating the payoff is based on the implied promise of sustainability: you assume the same level of pleasure – maybe even better next time, but the promise is empty. Repetition has diminishing returns and becomes a vexing habit. These actions are clearly not in your best interest.

2. Emotional health

Emotions are not bad. They are God-given and serve important purposes. Their sheer power, however, makes them a double-edged sword. Fear can save your life or make it miserable; it can make you run to safety or immobilize you.

Anger, which is not a primary emotion but is usually a reaction to fear or injury, can motivate you to right a wrong or to compound it and make it worse.

Revenge, so delicious in the planning, creates a never-ending cycle of new offenses that fail to deliver peace. Instead, it destroys any hope of peace. Actions that undermine your emotional health are clearly not in your best interest.

3. Psychological health

Psychology, according to the American Psychological Association, is the study of the mind and behavior.

Your mind governs the interaction of your rational and emotional faculties, resulting in the stories you tell yourself to "understand" your past and present. You may use these stories to self-medicate feelings of guilt and shame. You may also use them to convince yourself that you have value and are worthy of love.

When the stories align with objective truth, they can be very helpful. When the stories are flawed, they become counterproductive, preventing healthy self-worth and leading to many kinds of dysfunction. Actions that undermine your psychological health are clearly not in your best interest.

4. Spiritual health

What is your spirit? This is perhaps the biggest mystery of all. Ask ten theologians and you will probably get at least twenty different answers.

Many will agree, however, that the spirit of a human being is our central core, the part of us that is most receptive to the Spirit of God. Some say, "I am a spirit; I have a soul; I live in a body." If your spirit is your core, the essence of you that has the closest possible contact with God, its value cannot be overstated.

Damaging your spirit short-circuits your potential to hear and respond to God's voice. Actions as simple as overriding your conscience undermine spiritual health and are clearly not in your best interest.

Personal inventory

Given all of this, are you aware of occasional actions or patterns or even habits that are not in your best interest? Have you realized yet that something is driving these actions?

Whether you chalk it up to ignorance, immaturity, some kind of imbalance, or a spiritual force (the devil made me do it), it is clear that something needs to change.

Is self-denial the answer?

Jesus talked about a kind of self-denial that leads to peace by killing off our old fallen nature in favor of the new creation we become through second birth. *"And he said to all, 'If anyone would come after me, let him deny himself and take up his cross daily and follow me. For whoever would save his life will lose it, but whoever loses his life for my sake will save it. For what does it profit a man if he gains the whole world and loses or forfeits himself?'"* (Luke 9:23-25, ESV).

Peter notes the reality of the second birth: *"According to his great mercy, he has caused us to be **born again** to a living hope through the resurrection of Jesus Christ from the dead"* (1 Peter 1:3, ESV, emphasis added).

Other religions have a different approach to attaining peace through self-denial. Buddhists and New Age spiritualists hope to find peace by achieving Nirvana, a word derived from the Sanskrit that means extinction or disappearance of the individual to the universal.

This idea of blending into the universal sounds ultimately satisfying, which is why many, even in our western culture, are drawn to it. The Oxford Dictionary defines it as "a transcendent state in which there is neither suffering, desire, nor sense of self, and the subject is released from the effects of karma and the cycle of death and rebirth. It represents the final goal of Buddhism."

Although this goal sounds attractive, it has destruction of the self at its heart. It is not an opportunity to consciously live in complete harmony with everything that exists. Rather, it is an attempt to experience peace through the disciplined killing of all personal desires.

In a nutshell, if you have no desire, you have no disappointments. Pursuing this to the highest level, you become increasingly inert, caring for nothing beyond your longing to cease existence as a self and surrender to the universe. When achieved (in death) you will no longer feel, think, or exist as a unique being. "You" simply cease to exist.

This is directly at odds with the kind of self-denial Jesus talked about. Far from the destruction of your unique essence as a consciously aware individual, Jesus promises a transformation that enables you to become your best self – a self that bears his image for all eternity.

In heaven you will be the perfected you, living in harmony with all around you while still retaining your unique personality and identity – the one-of-a-kind creation God designed you to be. His provision of peace for his children in their eternal home elevates us to the status of joint heirs with Christ. This is the final goal of Christianity.

Inner peace
Until then, the time when you are united forever with Christ, you have the opportunity to experience the unfailing peace of God – even in this fallen world. The prophet Isaiah described it this way, *"You will keep in perfect peace all who trust in you, all whose thoughts are fixed on you!"* (Isaiah 26:3, NLT).

In the New Testament, Jesus promised, *"I am leaving you with a gift – peace of mind and heart. And the peace I give is a gift the world cannot give. So don't be troubled or afraid"* (John 14:27, NLT).

In both cases, we have a role to play. Isaiah describes the recipients of this peace as *"all who trust in you, all whose thoughts are fixed on you!"*

Jesus follows the announcement of his gift of peace with a command for us to obey: *"don't be troubled or afraid."* God promises to do his part, but we must do ours.

Inner peace is about security. It doesn't imply the absence of pain, but it interprets pain in a way that makes it more tolerable. Rather than denying reality, it recognizes a larger reality beyond the moment – an ultimate beneficial conclusion provided for us by the one who conquered death.

Inner peace includes qualities like a sense of safety in the storm, tranquility, contentment, and confidence. It is a form of wealth that money can't buy. In some ways, it's like water or air: you desperately need it even though you rarely think about it.

Alignment with reality (Truth)

The path to lasting peace is to align yourself with reality as completely and constantly as possible. By "reality," I mean absolute, enduring truth revealed by the ultimate authority, the God of the Bible and creator of all that exists.

Aligning yourself with reality means redefining your worldview with pillars of timeless truth. Only these can form and support a reliable intuition to guide you in today's complex and fast-paced world. They progressively overhaul flawed assumptions with improved ones that act as guardrails for your thinking, emotions, and decisions.

This conscious process brings increased awareness of God's presence in every moment of your life. His presence with you includes his massive power to transform you into the unique and amazing person he created you to be.

The reason for creating this Peace Credo

If this alignment process sounds complicated and discouraging, you've put your finger on the reason for creating the Peace Credo. It simplifies the process by identifying foundational essentials of inner peace. Increasing your awareness of God's 24/7 presence, it's like opening the door of your home to the expert craftsman who renovates as you continue with other daily responsibilities.

6

Meet the Peace Credo

As Maria (my wife) and I worked to reprogram our minds, we created a memorable credo that we could easily repeat throughout the day to tune our hearts to the unfailing peace and abundant life God offers us.

The Peace Credo's overall purpose is not to replace Scripture but to get it from our heads into our hearts, from concept into action, from afterthought to habit of choice.

We decided it should incorporate five crucial components:

1. **God's identity** – the ultimate truth and eternal reality
2. **My identity** – who I am from God's perspective
3. **Trust** – the active faith I need to be in relationship with God
4. **Gratitude** – the expression of trust in God's identity, purpose, and plan
5. **Action** – practical applications

We settled on seven short statements. Easy to memorize and repeat, they are guardrails for renewing our minds. Taking only forty seconds to recite at a comfortable pace, we pray them from memory the first thing every morning and the last thing at night. We also pray them throughout the day – as often as God prompts the thought.

But simply repeating the seven statements of the Peace Credo provides no value if it is not accompanied by conscious consideration and application. Think through the implications of God's identity, your identity, how trust and gratitude work, and how inner peace is achieved.

For Memory

7 lines, 75 words, 40 seconds

1. You, the Creator of everything, are Sovereign, Providential, and Redemptive.
2. I am your loved child, redeemed by the blood of Jesus Christ and being transformed daily.
3. I choose to trust you and your plan before understanding it.
4. Thank you for your good plan and how you are working it out in my life.
5. Repenting of all known sin, I choose to live fully forgiven.
6. I forgive everyone for everything.
7. I cast every care on you.

Thoughtfully repeating this multiple times every day helps us focus on God's reality rather than Satan's deceptions. For these truths to transform our thinking, we need to explore their implications and depth of meaning. This happens as we examine them word by word, which is the essence of godly meditation.

As you can see, the statements are very condensed. Every word counts. Many key words deserve a close look to appreciate their full significance. The more you meditate on each element, the more meaningful the whole thing becomes.

Consider this brief amplified version as an introduction to unpacking the depth and value of the Peace Credo for meditation. The **bold words are the Peace Credo itself.** [Everything in brackets is explanatory content.]

For meditation [Amplified Version]

1. You, the Creator [Designer and Sustainer] **of everything** [seen and unseen, the entire universe including anything that preceded it or will succeed it], **are Sovereign** [the ultimate and sole authority with unlimited power to accomplish your comprehensive plan], **Providential** [actively working – often behind the scenes – to do good on our behalf], **and Redemptive** [transforming our polluted hearts and using even our mistakes to bring about a good result].

2. I am your loved [not because I am worthy but because you *are* love] **child** [adopted into your holy family as a joint heir with Christ], **redeemed by the blood of Jesus Christ** [bought back from slavery to the enemy] **and being transformed** [from a polluted, fallen creature to the image of your Son] **daily** [little by little, one step at a time].

3. I choose [a conscious act of my will] **to trust** [have confidence in and rely on] **you** [your trustworthiness regardless of my temporary circumstances] **and your plan** [determined and guaranteed before creation] **before understanding it** [I can (and must) trust many things I don't yet understand. Your plan included a cross for Christ. By faith I accept trusting before understanding because I have learned that trust and obedience precede and enable understanding.]

4. **Thank you** [my happiness is dependent upon my gratitude and cannot exceed it] **for your good plan** [perfectly reflecting your creative power, unfailing love, and patient character in working all things together for good] **and how you are working it out** [providentially bringing it to pass] **in my life** [and simultaneously everyone else's].

5. **Repenting of** [confessing and turning away from] **all known sin, I choose to live fully forgiven.** [I forgive myself and reject the shame of the enemy's obsolete accusations by trusting completely in the grace of your forgiveness that enables me to live victoriously.]

6. **I forgive everyone for everything** [No exceptions. All forgiveness – including the forgiveness I have received from you – is undeserved].

7. **I cast** [and do not take back] **every care** [fear, concern, worry, hope, dream, aspiration] **on you** [with your unlimited resources and perfect master plan].

Difficulty memorizing the seven lines?
Here is an easy to remember shortcut. Try memorizing the first word of each line. It's a simple pattern you can divide in the middle to make it even easier. Two tiny sentences.

"You, I, I, Thank. Repenting, I, I."

You, the Creator of everything, are Sovereign, Providential, and Redemptive.

I am your loved child, redeemed by the blood of Jesus Christ and being transformed daily.

I choose to trust you and your plan before understanding it.

Thank you for your good plan and how you are working it out in my life.

Repenting of all known sin, I choose to live fully forgiven.

I forgive everyone for everything.

I cast every care on you.

Remember that the first two lines are identity statements. The third is trust, and the fourth is gratitude. The last three lines are confessions of obedience in response to the first four.

The logic of this organization combined with the pattern of these first words, "You, I, I, Thank. Repenting, I, I." should speed your memorization.

And the necessary repetition is not merely an unfortunate learning curve: you get to double dip, because it's actually growing your awareness and trust even as you do the work of memorizing.

7

God's Identity – the Foundation for Everything

You, the Creator of everything, are Sovereign, Providential, and Redemptive.
I am your loved child, redeemed by the blood of Jesus Christ and being transformed daily.
I choose to trust you and your plan before understanding it.
Thank you for your good plan and how you are working it out in my life.
Repenting of all known sin, I choose to live fully forgiven.
I forgive everyone for everything.
I cast every care on you.

What constitutes identity? Of all the factors we could consider, which are important to our worldview? To answer the question, let's begin the exploration in more familiar territory. Who are you?

What could be easier to ask and more difficult to answer? When asked, we usually respond by giving our name, but our name alone is rarely sufficient to satisfy someone who doesn't know us – especially if they don't know why we have come to see them.

A multitude of follow-up questions hover in their mind, questions like, why are you here? or, who sent you? The questions they actually ask are usually less direct – asked more politely – but they are still designed to size us up and help them determine whether we should be considered a help, a threat, or irrelevant.

What they really want to know is, can I trust you? That question is the primary subtext in virtually all communication. It isn't asked directly, of course, because if we were not trustworthy, we would probably lie about it anyway. But they want to know.

So, they ask less direct questions to get a feel for our attitude in general, or they may wait to see and assess evidence from our actions. Even among close friends, the ongoing process of calibrating trust operates constantly in the background of our intuition.

Whether they feel they can trust us is likely to depend on the answers they piece together from two additional questions lurking in their mind: (1) Do you care about me? (2) Do you know what you are doing (are you competent)?

The point is that our identity goes far beyond physical details like fingerprints, dental charts, eye scans, or Social Security numbers that distinguish us from the billions of people on the planet who are *not* us.

At the core of the "Who are you?" question is the relational significance that the questioner *really* wants to know: Who are you *to me*? Or, How should I relate to you?

All of this is at the heart of our questions about God: does he care, and does he have power? If he exists and if he is responsible for our existence, it logically follows that how we relate to him is vitally important. His nature and intentions define everything.

To the degree that we misunderstand his nature and intentions, we will be fundamentally wrong in our perceptions about the world and its meaning. Does he desire to hurt us or to help us? Is he capable of accomplishing his desire? How do we find out?

Science, by definition, is limited to the domain of the physical. Since God cannot be perceived by our physical senses, science is incapable of answering the question of his existence. Our search for God must include metaphysical evidence, but that doesn't make it wishful thinking or relegate it to faulty logic and sloppy analysis.

Cause and effect

Because the universe consistently demonstrates the law of cause and effect, we conclude that every effect has a cause. This enables astronomers to deduce the existence of an invisible cause, a black hole for example, because of the effects it has on the objects around it. Although the cause cannot be directly observed, we know that logic demands its existence because of the effects it causes.

Closer to home, we have observed that gravity is the cause of things falling to the ground, but we cannot see, hear, taste, smell, or feel it. We have logically deduced and empirically verified that it is an inherent property in all physical objects and is proportional to their mass.

In summary, some causes are obvious, but others are invisible (like God) and have to be logically deduced.

First Cause

In our attempts to understand our origins, we trace effects and their preceding causes backward as far as we can go, leading us to the Big Bang. Science, limited to the physical, theorizes that energy and matter have always existed in some form. The Big Bang may have been the physical cause of the universe, but the infinitely dense Singularity preceding the Big Bang has no explanation as to its origin.

At this point, we are forced to choose among seemingly impossible alternatives. Either everything came from nothing (spontaneous generation – no logical cause) or something (a First Cause) has always existed.

Although we cannot comprehend something without a beginning – something that always existed – we are logically forced to accept the reality: *something* had to exist without beginning.

We do not attribute it, however, to a merely physical Singularity without consciousness or intent. The intricate design evident throughout the universe, the recurring themes, our own consciousness – including self-awareness, moral capacity, relational design, etc. – all of these argue for a Designer with both consciousness and intent.

Either conclusion – an unconscious, lifeless Singularity or a living God – requires faith. The Christian perspective is that the weight of evidence points to a Creator, a First Cause, who has always existed.

"Lift up your eyes and look to the heavens: Who created all these? He who brings out the starry host one by one and calls forth each of them by name. Because of his great power and mighty strength, not one of them is missing" (Isaiah 40:26, NIV).

Speaking of Jesus as the Creator, John begins his Gospel with these words: *"In the beginning the Word already existed. The Word was with God, and the Word was God. ² He existed in the beginning with God. ³ God created everything through him, and nothing was created except through him. ⁴ The Word gave life to everything that was created, and his life brought light to everyone. ⁵ The light shines in the darkness, and the darkness can never extinguish it"* (John 1:1-5, NLT).

In the Judeo-Christian view, no one predated God. No one has a prior claim to creation or ownership. As the First Cause in God's chain of successive causes, all things find their reason for existence in him.

"You are worthy, our Lord and God, to receive glory and honor and power, for you created all things, and by your will they were created and have their being" (Revelation 4:11, NIV).

The First Cause has a name

We have no quarrel with science as far as it is able to take us. But when we come to the limits of its domain (the physical), we go where it cannot go – into the most logical explanation for the nonphysical ultimate First Cause. We call the First Cause by the generic name, God.

Many biblical names are attributed to him, the most notable being Jehovah, which is derived from Yahweh, the spoken version of the unpronounceable YHWH. Theologians define YHWH as "He Brings into Existence Whatever Exists."

When God got Moses' attention through a burning bush and commissioned him to the seemingly impossible task of convincing Pharaoh to release the Hebrews, Moses wanted to know what authority was behind the orders.

Moses' question in modern language would go something like this: "Are you serious? Before I ever get to Pharaoh, I have to convince my own people that you are behind this. I don't know where to begin. What did you say your name is?"

God's response was, *"I AM who I AM. Say to the people of Israel, 'I AM has sent me to you.'"*

When we reflect on this strange name, we are struck by two major concepts: (1) God is infinite (beyond description or measure) and (2) eternal (timeless and unchanging). Every imaginable description falls short. He exceeds every measurement or boundary. Before the universe was, *"I AM."* After the universe ceases to be, *"I AM."*

To this uncaused First Cause, the eternal *"I AM,"* *everything* else owes its existence. And it is only in relationship to *"I AM"* that every living being is defined and finds its ultimate purpose.

This is why our Peace Credo begins with God's identity before moving to our own. We could, of course, in our typically self-centered human way, begin with our identity but we wouldn't get far before having to retreat. Since we are the Effect of a Cause beyond ourselves, we can hardly define ourselves without recognizing that Cause and our relationship to it.

8

God's Identity – Creator

You, the **Creator** of everything . . .

You, the Creator of everything, are Sovereign, Providential, and Redemptive.
I am your loved child, redeemed by the blood of Jesus Christ and being transformed daily.
I choose to trust you and your plan before understanding it.
Thank you for your good plan and how you are working it out in my life.
Repenting of all known sin, I choose to live fully forgiven.
I forgive everyone for everything.
I cast every care on you.

Can you imagine the power and wisdom of the one who created everything that exists? Just the ability to create a single human being is mind boggling. The more you know of our physiology, the more absurdly amazing it becomes. And we are a tiny speck on the planet, which is a speck in the solar system, which is a tiny speck in the galaxy, which is . . . endless.

"In the beginning, God created the heavens and the earth" (Genesis 1:1, ESV).

"God, the Lord, created the heavens and stretched them out. He created the earth and everything in it. He gives breath to everyone, life to everyone who walks the earth" (Isaiah 42:5, NLT).

Every now and then – especially when I am outdoors and aware of my surroundings – a strange question ambushes me: How can all of this be real? It makes me laugh when I think of countless competing and opposing forces – from weather extremes to daily cycles of light and dark, to the gases in the air we breathe, the natural competition within species as well as beyond, the sun's gravity that holds the earth in orbit and the earth's gravity that holds its inhabitants on the surface – all of these somehow coexist in relative balance.

A follow-up question immediately challenges: How can it *not* be real? My senses are experiencing it, my brain is processing it. The trees, the birds, the breeze, the grass, the cars, the people driving them – each of whom has his own perspective and worldview – these are not just in my imagination; they are real. Then comes the ultimate head scratcher: How and why does all of this exist? Some see this question as meaningless; I do not.

Maybe I'm weird, but my guess is that many of us have such thoughts. We see unimaginable complexity, from the astronomic (think billions of galaxies) to the microscopic (think DNA).

God claims the astronomic in his words through the prophet Isaiah, *"It is I who made the earth and created mankind on it. My own hands stretched out the heavens; I marshaled their starry hosts"* (Isaiah 45:12, NIV).

Then he moves to the microscopic in the words of the psalmist, *"For you created my inmost being; you knit me together in my mother's womb"* (Psalm 139:13, NIV).

But our heads spin at the implications of so many conflicting realities: indescribable beauty alongside enormous pain and suffering; the inevitability of nature's physical laws – which we cannot violate – in contrast to moral laws that we insist are valid while we consistently violate them.

The Christian conclusion is that the weight of evidence agrees with the Bible's revelations of a personal God who created all of it as a display of his character. Declaring all of it "good," he put his stamp of approval on humankind, declaring it "*very* good."

Further, he risked granting them free will, enabling them to return his love and fully enjoy the blessings of paradise – or rebel against him and suffer the consequences of cutting themselves off from his full blessing.

The fly in the ointment

Choosing anything other than complete obedience to God's character and plan is to choose something less than perfect. However slight the imperfection at the outset, over time it infects everything around it, creating abscesses in what was once healthy tissue.

The consequences of departing from perfection increase exponentially as more and more infected cells reproduce their damaged identity. We know from daily experience that God's "good" creation has gone unmistakably off the rails – at least as far as humankind is concerned. We chose (and continue to choose) to rebel. We endure the inevitable consequences.

Our dilemma is that we want free will without consequences. Unfortunately, that imaginary state is a self-contradiction, a logical impossibility even for God. Real choices lead to real actions that inevitably have real consequences. Even God cannot remove consequences without violating the free will he has given us. A choice with no consequences is meaningless, effectively no choice at all.

Free will within boundaries

Instead, he has taken a different approach. By placing natural boundaries on our free will, he mitigates the damage we produce by limiting our powers to operate.

First, the nature of our physical bodies limits us to actions within dimensional space: we cannot be physically present in more than one space at a time.

Second, we are limited to sequential, dimensional time: we cannot be present in more than one moment at a time. Nor can we time-travel to create havoc in more than one moment at a time.

Third, we are limited in brain capacity and the amount of knowledge we can employ to hurt one another. Super computers and artificial intelligence are beginning to stretch that boundary, raising the question of a future tower of Babel to slow us down.

Fourth, we are limited in lifespan. The reason God ejected Adam and Eve from the Garden was to prevent the unthinkable nightmare of immortal existence in a fallen state – what would have been a nightmare to Adam and Eve themselves as well as to those they and their offspring would harm.

"And the Lord God said, 'The man has now become like one of us, knowing good and evil. He must not be allowed to reach out his hand and take also from the tree of life and eat, and live forever.' [23] *So the Lord God banished him from the Garden of Eden to work the*

ground from which he had been taken. ²⁴ After he drove the man out, he placed on the east side of the Garden of Eden cherubim and a flaming sword flashing back and forth to guard the way to the tree of life" (Genesis 3:22-24, NIV).

This was not a simple punishment for Adam's disobedience; it was also a protection from living forever as a being with a moral conscience that he would continuously violate. Immortality in our fallen condition would not be a welcome escape from death; it would be a never-ending death trap.

I think there is also a correlation between the long lifespans before the Flood and the much shorter lifespans thereafter. God's reset button did more than simply destroy the earth's ultra-evil inhabitants; it also limited the length of time any human could continue to accumulate power and breed devastation.

Should God have granted free will?

All of this raises the question: Given the grave risks, should God have created man with moral capacity and free will?

First, we must realize that any human answer to this question is hardly authoritative. To angels and higher powers with a more expansive view of God's character and plan, our answer probably doesn't even reach the level of meaningful. I can imagine them responding like Isaiah: *"Do you not know? Have you not heard? The Lord is the everlasting God, the Creator of the ends of the earth. He will not grow tired or weary, and his understanding no one can fathom"* (Isaiah 40:28, NIV).

Since we cannot fathom the depth of his understanding, we tend to move pretty quickly to our own personal level, where the question looks more like this: Is it better for me to have lived than never to have lived at all?

Every day my actions vote yes to this question, even though I may not consciously consider it. I have the free will to end my own existence if I think it is not worth living. Apparently, there is a hope embedded deeply within me that believes the good I can experience outweighs the bad. And the good news of the gospel is that even the bad can be redeemed through faith in God's gift of love and grace through his Son.

So, as a philosophical consideration, the question of whether God should have granted free will may seem perplexing, but as a pragmatic daily choice, it's crystal clear: we continually vote yes by our choice to keep living.

Perhaps that choice to keep living is fragile for you right now. If something has caused you to feel hopeless, you are experiencing the deepest, darkest moments of your life. They feel as though they will never end; that's the nature of hopelessness. Stay with us and try to open your mind to the possibility that God has a new door, a good future for you – one in which your despair will yield to greater insight, meaning, and even joy. The God who designed you can bring healing and *"repay you for the years the locusts have eaten"* (Joel 2:25, NIV).

God's choice to give us free will is a two-edged gift: it can be destructive, but love cannot be expressed without it. God chose to express love and to give us the same opportunity.

His plan to conquer the problem of our failure and the suffering we have caused involves multiple actions. (1) He took the consequences upon himself through the substitutionary death of Christ. (2) He granted us an unearned righteousness by grace through faith in what Christ accomplished for us on the cross. (3) He incorporated our unrighteous acts into the rich fabric of his plan, using them to demonstrate the triumph of love and grace over naked justice (using for good what Satan meant for evil). (4) He adopted us into his family and rewarded us with *eternal* life free of pain and regret – a windfall trade for the suffering we experience during our eye blink of an earthly lifetime.

"God, for whom and through whom everything was made, chose to bring many children into glory. And it was only right that he should make Jesus, through his suffering, a perfect leader, fit to bring them into their salvation" (Hebrews 2:10, NLT).

This is God, the creator of everything, using the free will of his Son to remake our corrupted free will. And this remake is available to all who surrender their wills to him.

9

God's Identity – Sovereign

You, the Creator of everything, are **Sovereign**

You, the Creator of everything, are Sovereign, Providential, and Redemptive.
I am your loved child, redeemed by the blood of Jesus Christ and being transformed daily.
I choose to trust you and your plan before understanding it.
Thank you for your good plan and how you are working it out in my life.
Repenting of all known sin, I choose to live fully forgiven.
I forgive everyone for everything.
I cast every care on you.

God is before all. No one tells him what to do. No one limits his power. No one can prevent his good will from accomplishing his good plan. All else finds its place within his blueprint, serves its purpose within his plan, and bends its knee at his command. Even Satan.

"The Lord has established His throne in the heavens, And His sovereignty rules over all" (Psalm 103:19, NASB).

As Creator of everything, God's sovereignty is logically self-evident. If everyone is a created being that owes their existence to him, no one can meaningfully challenge his sovereign authority. *"You alone are the Lord. You made the skies and the heavens and all the stars. You made the earth and the seas and everything in them. You preserve them all, and the angels of heaven worship you"* (Nehemiah 9:6, NLT).

Sovereign covenants
Noah witnessed God's sovereignty in a profound way. He saw God exercise his right to obliterate a creation gone bad and start again.

He also witnessed God's covenant: *"'I establish my covenant with you, that never again shall all flesh be cut off by the waters of the flood, and never again shall there be a flood to destroy the earth.' And God said, 'This is the sign of the covenant that I make between me and you and every living creature that is with you, for all future generations: I have set my bow in the cloud, and it shall be a sign of the covenant between me and the earth'"* (Genesis 9:11-13, ESV).

This remarkable passage is the first mention of any covenant between the earth's inhabitants and its sovereign God. God makes additional covenants, however, as a means of revealing his holy nature and restoring fallen mankind. We initially accept them with gratitude and enthusiasm. *"Sovereign Lord, you are God! Your covenant is trustworthy, and you have promised these good things to your servant"* (2 Samuel 7:28, NIV).

But then, of course, we revert to our old ways and violate every promise we have made. In spite of our failures and in spite of his sovereign power to do as he wishes, God never goes back on his word. *"So when God desired to show more convincingly to the heirs of the promise the unchangeable character of his purpose, he guaranteed it with an oath, so that by two* *unchangeable things, in which **it is impossible for God to lie**, we who have fled for refuge might have strong encouragement to hold fast to the hope set before us"* (Hebrews 6:17-18, ESV, emphasis added).

"It is impossible for God to lie" because he is the truth. When his covenants, intended to bind us to himself, are broken and abandoned by our corrupt willfulness, God opens yet another door. This time it is one that is infinitely costly – to him.

We are the beneficiaries of God's new covenant through the blood of Christ. *"He will swallow up death forever. The **Sovereign** Lord will wipe away the tears from all faces; he will remove his people's disgrace from all the earth. The Lord has spoken. In that day they will say, 'Surely this is our God; we trusted in him, and he saved us. This is the Lord, we trusted in him; let us rejoice and be glad in his salvation'"* (Isaiah 25:8-9, NIV, emphasis added).

Prime Mover

Although this designation is generally a synonym for First Cause, we're using it here in an additional sense. Beyond being the First Cause, God continues to interact with his creation as he works out his sovereign plan. Having chosen to grant free will to his creatures in spite of the consequences, he continues to hold all of creation together within predetermined boundaries to achieve his intended outcomes.

*"The Son is the image of the invisible God, the firstborn over all creation. For **in him all things were created:** things in heaven and on earth, visible and invisible, whether thrones or powers or rulers or*

*authorities; all things have been created through him and for him. He is before all things, and **in him all things hold together***" (Colossians 1:15-17, NIV, emphasis added).

The laws of physics testify to God's intelligent design and his desire to reveal himself as creative, orderly, logical, dependable, in control of the expanse of the universe, and bigger than life itself.

The moral law he has put into the conscience of all humankind (that we should love him and love one another as we love ourselves) testifies to his goodness, care, and mercy.

The Prime Mover influencing our free will from within

God has taken yet another major step as Prime Mover. He has deposited a part of himself within every person who trusts Jesus, the Son, as savior. The Holy Spirit helps us to move in accordance with the Father's plan. He enlightens and influences our free will to move in ways that are far better for us than we would otherwise choose – or could even imagine.

"That is what the Scriptures mean when they say, 'No eye has seen, no ear has heard, and no mind has imagined what God has prepared for those who love him.' But it was to us that God revealed these things by his Spirit. For his Spirit searches out everything and shows us God's deep secrets" (1 Corinthians 2:9-10, NLT).

Jesus knew that his followers (including us) would need frequent reminding of his teachings as long as we live in a world filled with deceptive messages.

Before he ascended into heaven, he promised that the Father would send the Holy Spirit to us. *"But the Helper, the Holy Spirit, whom the Father will send in my name, he will teach you all things and bring to your remembrance all that I have said to you"* (John 14:26, ESV).

The Holy Spirit within us not only reminds and teaches but also guides us into all truth. *"When the Spirit of truth comes, he will guide you into all the truth, for he will not speak on his own authority, but whatever he hears he will speak, and he will declare to you the things that are to come. He will glorify me, for he will take what is mine and declare it to you"* (John 16:13-14, ESV).

God, as Prime Mover, takes the initiative through his Spirit within us to help us as he strengthens us and intercedes for us. Romans 8:26-27 says, *"And the Holy Spirit helps us in our weakness. For example, we don't know what God wants us to pray for. But the Holy Spirit prays for us with groanings that cannot be expressed in words. And the Father who knows all hearts knows what the Spirit is saying, for the Spirit pleads for us believers in harmony with God's own will"* (NLT).

After pleading for us in harmony with God's own will, the Spirit becomes a personal manufacturing plant on our behalf. *"The Holy Spirit produces this kind of fruit in our lives: love, joy, peace, patience, kindness, goodness, faithfulness, gentleness, and self-control"* (Galatians 5:22-23, NLT). Isn't this what we all want when we stop and think about it?

God, as Sovereign Prime Mover, is ready to produce these qualities in you to the degree that you will open the door to him. In Revelation 3:20 God says, *"Look! I have been standing at the door, and I am constantly knocking. If anyone hears me calling him and opens the door, I will come in and fellowship with him and he with me"* (TLB).

And we see the result in Colossians 1:10, *"Then the way you live will always honor and please the Lord, and your lives will produce every kind of good fruit. All the while, you will grow as you learn to know God better and better"* (NLT).

Ultimate Authority
No one tells God what to do.

No one has the power to give God orders. Every authority on earth (and beyond) is delegated by God in accordance with his purpose and plan. Each can appeal to (and will be judged by) a higher authority. God is the lone exception because there is no higher authority. Hebrews 6:13 says, *"For example, there was God's promise to Abraham. Since there was no one greater to swear by, God took an oath in his own name"* (NLT).

God says through Isaiah, *"'To whom will you compare me? Or who is my equal?' says the Holy One"* (Isaiah 40:25 NIV).

No one has the moral authority to call him to account. The prophet Daniel says, *"All the people of the earth are nothing compared to him. He does as he pleases among the angels of heaven and among the people of the earth. No one can stop him or say to* him, 'What do you mean by doing these things?'" (Daniel 4:35, NLT).

Fortunately, there is no need to call him to account, because he is above temptation. *". . . God cannot be tempted with evil, and he himself tempts no one"* (James 1:13, ESV).

*"Acknowledge and take to heart this day that **the Lord is God in heaven above and on the earth below. There is no other.** Keep his decrees and commands, which I am giving you today, so that it may go well with you and your children after you and that you may live long in the land the Lord your God gives you for all time"* (Deuteronomy 4:39-40, NIV, emphasis added).

"Yours, O Lord, is the greatness, the power, the glory, the victory, and the majesty. Everything in the heavens and on earth is yours, O Lord, and this is your kingdom. We adore you as the one who is over all things" (1 Chronicles 29:11, NLT).

10

God's Identity – Providential

You, the Creator of everything, are Sovereign, **Providential, . . .**

> You, the Creator of everything, are Sovereign, Providential, and Redemptive.
> I am your loved child, redeemed by the blood of Jesus Christ and being transformed daily.
> I choose to trust you and your plan before understanding it.
> Thank you for your good plan and how you are working it out in my life.
> Repenting of all known sin, I choose to live fully forgiven.
> I forgive everyone for everything.
> I cast every care on you.

"Providential" is an adjective describing acts that involve divine foresight and intervention. Its Latin root is the present participle of prōvidēre ("to provide"). Hailing back to the fourteenth century, the English word "Providence" meant "God's beneficial care or guidance."

Even in the middle of Job's complaints and questioning of God, he acknowledges God's providence. *"You have granted me life and loving-kindness; And Your providence [divine care, supervision] has preserved my spirit"* (Job 10:12, AMP).

In theology, Providence is God's intervention in the universe. *"The eyes of all look to You, and You give them their food in due time. You open Your hand and satisfy the desire of every living thing"* (Psalm 145:15-16, NASB).

"God is our refuge and strength, an ever-present help in trouble" (Psalm 46:1, NIV).

An important component in God's identity is that he does only good, all the time. He is at work behind the scenes, often without our awareness or gratitude, and always on our behalf. *"The Lord is righteous in all His ways and kind in all His works"* (Psalm 145:17, NASB). *"For I am the Lord your God who takes hold of your right hand and says to you, Do not fear; I will help you"* (Isaiah 41:13, NIV).

God's providence is judiciously active

Giving and receiving love are impossible without free will. But free will also gives us the means to hurt each other when we are not in harmony with God's character and his will for us.

Fallen humanity frequently accuses God of doing either too much or too little. In good times, we wish he would stay out of our way and leave us to our own devices. In bad times, we wish he wouldn't be so slow to give us what we want. Clearly, our wishes in any given moment dictate our perception of whether God is doing his job well as Chief Providential Officer.

Why does God not do more? Why does he not intervene with frequent miracles to prevent unjust pain and suffering? We don't realize that we often ask God to do the intrinsically impossible. How can he honor us with free will and withhold it at the same time?

If God disarmed people every time they started to act in a violent way, he would be forever suspending the laws of nature. Should bullets flying through the air suddenly slow down and become water drops? Should a fist turn to jelly before landing on someone's jaw? Always or only in certain instances? Would we then be exerting our own will or someone else's?

This level of interference in our fixed environment would prevent us from operating freely and so restrict our choices that our actions would have little meaning.

How does God resolve this dilemma? One way is to limit our time on this fallen planet so that it is hardly even a moment in view of eternity. Another is to prepare an eternal place for us that is beyond our imagination. In light of these, Paul tells us in 2 Corinthians 4:17 that *"our present troubles are small and won't last very long. Yet they produce for us a glory that vastly outweighs them and will last forever!"* (NLT).

These two answers have little impact on us because of our physical constraints. We have firsthand experience with only this lifetime. Because it is all we know, it is difficult to think beyond its boundaries. This often yields a pragmatic philosophy that says, "you only go around once in life, so you have to grab for all the gusto you can get," in other words, this is all there is.

Against that backdrop, any talk of a bigger picture, an eternal existence, seems like a meaningless fairy tale. But if a bigger picture actually exists outside of our immediate senses, it changes everything. And once we have experienced it, our former ignorance will strike us as painfully obvious.

God's providence helps us think and choose

God's providence also means that he has not left us to figure it out on our own. He didn't speak the universe into existence and then simply step back to watch how it would play out. His wisdom and foreknowledge, motivated by love, intervene constantly in our lives.

Most of the time it is subtle, as his Spirit whispers in our thoughts to teach and remind us. Jesus made a point of this when he told the disciples, *"But the Advocate, the Holy Spirit, whom the Father will send in my name, will teach you all things and will remind you of everything I have said to you"* (John 14:26, NIV).

He influences our thinking while leaving us free to decide our actions. *"For it is God who works in you to will and to act in order to fulfill his good purpose"* (Philippians 2:13, NIV).

God's providence protects

Other times his intervention is more dramatic. You can probably recall multiple times when God has spared your life, likely with the aid of unseen angels. *"Angels are only servants – spirits sent to care for people who will inherit salvation"* (Hebrews 1:14, NLT).

"For the Angel of the Lord guards and rescues all who reverence him" (Psalm 34:7, TLB).

*"It was the Lord our God himself who brought us and our parents up out of Egypt, from that land of slavery, and performed those great signs before our eyes. He protected us on our entire journey and among

all the nations through which we traveled" (Joshua 24:17, NIV).

The psalmist frequently speaks of God's protection: *"You are my hiding place; you will protect me from trouble and surround me with songs of deliverance"* (Psalm 32:7, NIV).

"Oh, put God to the test and see how kind he is! See for yourself the way his mercies shower down on all who trust in him" (Psalm 34:8, TLB).

Jesus prayed to the Father on our behalf before he made the ultimate sacrifice for us. *"My prayer is not that you take them out of the world but that you protect them from the evil one"* (John 17:15, NIV). This, too, is part of God's providential plan for us.

Paul, knowing that Jesus prayed according to the will of the Father, echoes those words – not as a request but as a matter of fact. *"But the Lord is faithful, and he will strengthen you and protect you from the evil one"* (2 Thessalonians 3:3, NIV).

God's providence provides

"If you belong to the Lord, reverence him; for everyone who does this has everything he needs" (Psalm 34:9, TLB).

"And my God will meet all your needs according to the riches of his glory in Christ Jesus" (Philippians 4:19, NIV).

God's providence encourages

"Don't be afraid, for I am with you. Don't be discouraged, for I am your God. I will strengthen you and help you. I will hold you up with my victorious right hand" (Isaiah 41:10, NLT).

"The Lord is close to those whose hearts are breaking; he rescues those who are humbly sorry for their sins" (Psalm 34:18, TLB).

God's providence helps
"The Lord helps the fallen and lifts those bent beneath their loads" (Psalm 145:14, NLT).

"The good man does not escape all troubles—he has them too. But the Lord helps him in each and every one" (Psalm 34:19, TLB).

"In all your ways acknowledge Him, and He will make your paths straight" (Proverbs 3:6, NASB).

God's providence empowers
"He gives strength to the weary and increases the power of the weak" (Isaiah 40:29, NIV).

"The eyes of the Lord search the whole earth in order to strengthen those whose hearts are fully committed to him" (2 Chronicles 16:9, NLT).

"Wealth and honor come from you alone, for you rule over everything. Power and might are in your hand, and at your discretion people are made great and given strength" (1 Chronicles 29:12, NLT).

11

God's Identity – Redemptive

You, the Creator of everything, are Sovereign, Providential, and **Redemptive.**

> You, the Creator of everything, are Sovereign, Providential, and Redemptive.
> I am your loved child, redeemed by the blood of Jesus Christ and being transformed daily.
> I choose to trust you and your plan before understanding it.
> Thank you for your good plan and how you are working it out in my life.
> Repenting of all known sin, I choose to live fully forgiven.
> I forgive everyone for everything.
> I cast every care on you.

"But as for those who serve the Lord, he will redeem them; everyone who takes refuge in him will be freely pardoned" (Psalm 34:22, TLB).

"God shows his love for us in that while we were still sinners, Christ died for us" (Romans 5:8, ESV).

The good news of the gospel is that God is redemptive. When in spite of God's sovereign providence we rebel, we suffer consequences. We get kidnapped by the enemy, tortured, broken, and shamed for the very acts the enemy deceived us into committing.

But God pays our ransom – at the cost of Jesus' blood – to rescue us from slavery, restore our freedom, and repair our broken hearts.

Isaiah foretells God's plan for redemption: *"I have blotted out your transgressions like a cloud and your sins like mist; return to me, for I have redeemed you"* (Isaiah 44:22, ESV).

Paul, the former persecutor of Christians, confirms redemption through Jesus' blood. *"In him we have redemption through his blood, the forgiveness of our trespasses . . ."* (Ephesians 1:7-8, ESV).

And Jesus, even before the crucifixion, foretold his role in providing our redemption: *"For God so loved the world, that he gave his only Son, that whoever believes in him should not perish but have eternal life. For God did not send his Son into the world to condemn the world, but in order that the world might be saved through him"* (John 3:16-17, ESV).

God rescues

"Our God is a God who saves! The Sovereign Lord rescues us from death" (Psalm 97:10, NLT).

"The Lord rescues the godly; he is their fortress in times of trouble" (Psalm 37:39, NLT).

"For the Angel of the Lord guards and rescues all who reverence him" (Psalm 34:7, TLB).

In 1988, Maria and I recorded the song "A Rescuing God." It illustrates my personal experience with God's ongoing redemption, including the emotional desperation I feel before confessing, repenting, and receiving his full pardon.

The song didn't come on the heels of a particular crisis or dramatic turnaround; I had already been a committed follower of Christ for decades. Instead, it represents my frequent failure to walk fully in the

Spirit, to be holy. *"For the Scriptures say, 'You must be holy because I am holy'"* (1 Peter 1:16, NLT).

A RESCUING GOD

Oh, Lord, my soul longs for You
In this, my time of great need.
I fear You have left me alone;
There is no one who cares,
Who can answer my prayers,
Lord, I feel I am sinking like stone.
But, Lord, You've promised to hear when I cry out in prayer,
When I search for You with all my might.
So please hear me now in this hour of despair;
Turn my darkness into Your light.

Oh, Lord, my eyes can now see
The sin that I've hidden from You
The price that it's caused me to pay
All the pain and despair
Even sickness to bear
And the shame and reproach of this day.
But now I open my heart and I humbly repent
Of the sin I've committed against You
And for the time that I have so foolishly spent
In hiding from Your holy view.

You are a rescuing God, You are a saving Lord,
And You delight in the sound of Your children's praise;
You are a rescuing God, You are a saving Lord,
And I will praise Your name through all my days.

Lyrics and music by Steve Gardner © 1988 Aslan Family Music/ASCAP

"I trust in your unfailing love. I will rejoice because you have rescued me. I will sing to the Lord because he is good to me" (Psalm 13:5-6, NLT).

God's ability to use evil for good purposes
Beyond forgiving our sins and redeeming our souls, God even redeems and uses our failures. They become part of the rich tapestry he weaves to demonstrate the depth of his love and the unparalleled genius of his creativity.

And then, on top of it all, he invites us to share in his glory as though we somehow played a significant role in making the tapestry beautiful. *"And when Christ, who is your life, is revealed to the whole world, you will share in all his glory"* (Colossians 3:4, NLT).

In our discussion of "Providential," we raised the question, why does God not do more? His redemptive character is part of how he ***does*** do more – how he goes beyond mere protection to prepare us for future accomplishments. He uses even evil acts within our storyline to create a perfect ending. Rather than suspend our free will, he uses it in ways we cannot foresee or understand until much later – as with Joseph, whose jealous brothers sold him to slave traders.

Imagine Joseph's decades of trying to make sense of God's apparent lack of protection, how long he waits to see the bigger picture come into focus. Joseph's faithfulness in every situation where God places him results in his elevation to a position of power. His wisdom and foresight literally save the nation of Egypt along with many others, including his estranged family.

When famine forces Joseph's guilty brothers to travel to Egypt for grain, they are brought face to face with their long-lost brother. Terrified at the thought of the revenge he might take on them, they are unable to speak. Joseph has the power of life and death over them, but God had transformed his heart from that of a victim to that of a loving overcomer.

He acknowledges their sin while simultaneously declaring how God has used it for good. *"You intended to harm me, but God intended it all for good. He brought me to this position so I could save the lives of many people"* (Genesis 50:20, NLT).

Decades after the pain he suffered at the hands of his brothers, Joseph had the hard-earned privilege of seeing how God used evil for good. But even then he could never have guessed at the ramifications centuries later – how God would multiply his family into a great force and use the evil of a future Pharaoh to bring about the Exodus.

Passover

Even more prophetically powerful than the Exodus was the devastating tenth and final plague that caused Pharaoh to cave. We know it as the Passover because of the ingenious way God designed it to crush the enemy while sparing his own people.

The twelfth chapter of Exodus gives the story of his detailed instructions. They were far more strategic on many levels than the Israelites could have known at the time. In summary, they were to kill, roast, and eat a lamb after smearing some of its blood on their doorposts.

"For I will pass through the land of Egypt that night, and I will strike all the firstborn in the land of Egypt, both man and beast; and on all the gods of

Egypt I will execute judgments: I am the Lord. 13 The blood shall be a sign for you, on the houses where you are. And when I see the blood, I will **pass over** *you, and no plague will befall you to destroy you, when I strike the land of Egypt"* (Exodus 12:12-13, ESV, emphasis added).

This is how the observance of the Passover began. But it certainly didn't end there, because God had far more in mind than the simple release of Egypt's Israelite slaves. He didn't command them to just remember the Passover but to observe it every year *forever*.

"You shall observe this rite as a statute for you and for your sons forever. 25 And when you come to the land that the Lord will give you, as he has promised, you shall keep this service. 26And when your children say to you, 'What do you mean by this service?' 27 you shall say, 'It is the sacrifice of the Lord's **Passover,** *for he* **passed over** *the houses of the people of Israel in Egypt, when he struck the Egyptians but spared our houses'"* (Exodus 12:24-27, ESV, emphasis added).

This was so much more than a historic event to trigger the release of the Israelites: it was a foreshadowing of what God would do thirteen centuries later — on a much grander scale – involving all believers in his Son.

Jesus observed the Passover with his disciples on the night he was betrayed. On that night he became our Passover Lamb, commuting our death sentences through the power of his shed blood. *". . . For Christ, our Passover lamb, has been sacrificed"* (1 Corinthians 5:7, ESV).

That Passover evening, generally referred to as the Last Supper, is when Jesus instituted the ordinance of Holy Communion. When we take communion, we are reenacting a new version of the Passover, the new covenant confirmed by Jesus' blood. Jesus said, *"This is my blood, which confirms the covenant between God and his people. It is poured out as a sacrifice to forgive the sins of many"* (Matthew 26:28, NLT).

God using the ultimate evil for ultimate good

What could be more evil than Satan orchestrating the betrayal and crucifixion of God's only Son? Who could have guessed that God would allow Satan's free will to result is such a devastating act?

But what could be more good than the redemption of the world? And who could ever have imagined that God would use Satan's own evil choice as the means to reconcile the world to himself?

Paul further underscores the significance of Jesus' death used for good: *"For if, while we were God's enemies, we were reconciled to him through the death of his Son, how much more, having been reconciled, shall we be saved through his life!"* (Romans 5:10, NIV).

Although God's redemption is constantly at work behind the scenes, we don't have sufficient processing bandwidth to recognize more than a tiny fraction of it, including these benefits highlighted by the psalmist: *"He forgives all my sins and heals all my diseases. He redeems me from death and crowns me with love and tender mercies. He fills my life with good things. My youth is renewed like the eagle's!"* (Psalm 103:3-5, NLT).

12

My Identity – Loved

I am Your **loved** . . .

You, the Creator of everything, are Sovereign, Providential, and Redemptive.
I am your loved child, redeemed by the blood of Jesus Christ and being transformed daily.
I choose to trust you and your plan before understanding it.
Thank you for your good plan and how you are working it out in my life.
Repenting of all known sin, I choose to live fully forgiven.
I forgive everyone for everything.
I cast every care on you.

"We love because God loved us first" (1 John 4:19, CEV). *"There is no greater love than to lay down one's life for one's friends"* (John 15:13, NLT).

Love is all about the character of the lover, not the worthiness of the one loved. I can't claim to understand God's love, but I imagine that my love for my wife and children are a dim reflection of it. I certainly can't claim to deserve it, but I can receive it with gratitude as the beneficiary of its mystery.

The truth is that I AM loved, and nothing can separate me from the unfailing love of the Creator of everything. *". . . nothing in all creation will ever be able to separate us from the love of God that is revealed in Christ Jesus our Lord"* (Romans 8:39, NLT).

Even before God sent his son to die for us, he profusely declared his love through the prophets. *"The Lord appeared to us in the past, saying: 'I have loved you with an **everlasting love;** I have drawn you with* *unfailing kindness'"* (Jeremiah 31:3, NIV, emphasis added).

*"'Though the mountains be shaken and the hills be removed, yet my **unfailing love** for you will not be shaken nor my covenant of peace be removed,' says the Lord, who has compassion on you"* (Isaiah 54:10, NIV, emphasis added).

*"With your **unfailing love** you lead the people you have redeemed. In your might, you guide them to your sacred home"* (Exodus 15:13, NLT, emphasis added).

*"How precious is your **unfailing love**, O God! All humanity finds shelter in the shadow of your wings"* (Psalm 36:7, NLT, emphasis added).

*"Satisfy us in the morning with your **unfailing love**, that we may sing for joy and be glad all our days"* (Psalm 90:14, NIV, emphasis added).

Carefully read each phrase in this next passage to sense God's heart with regard to you. Look at what he is doing. *"For the Lord your God is living among you. He is a mighty savior. He will take delight in you with gladness. With his love, he will calm all your fears. He will rejoice over you with joyful songs"* (Zephaniah 3:17, NLT). Have you ever envisioned God singing over you with joy?

In case you've been interpreting these passages in light of God's love for humankind in general, take a moment to let the intense intimacy of this one sink in. You can't get more personal than this. *"You saw **me** before **I** was born. Every day of **my life** was recorded in your book. Every moment was laid out before a single day had passed. How precious are your thoughts about **me**, O God. They cannot be numbered!*

*I can't even count them; they outnumber the grains of sand! And when I wake up, you are still with **me!**"* (Psalm 139:16-19, NLT, emphasis added).

Blocking God's love

Sometimes we are our own worst enemy. Imagine God saying to you, "I wanted to protect you. I wanted you to enjoy the full benefits of my love, but you shut me out."

That's what Jesus was saying to Jerusalem as he grieved over the blindness and selfish hypocrisy of her religious leaders. *"O Jerusalem, Jerusalem, the city that kills the prophets and stones God's messengers! How often I have wanted to gather your children together as a hen protects her chicks beneath her wings, but you wouldn't let me"* (Matthew 23:37, NLT).

They took the law God gave his people to protect them and turned it into a self-serving weapon. Ignoring *"justice, mercy, and faith"* (Matthew 23:23), they piled on insufferable demands that they themselves did not follow. In doing so, they unwittingly insulated themselves from the love God wanted to lavish on them.

It's easy for us to see their sin and condemn it – confident that we would never do anything like that – without realizing how we do something very similar in our own context. Notice in Matthew 23:30 that Jesus says, *"Then you say, 'If we had lived in the days of our ancestors, we would never have joined them in killing the prophets.'"* His response to their claim fills much of the chapter and should be a sobering wakeup call to all of us.

Much of it has to do with practical behavior. The Golden Rule and honestly walking the talk are frequent themes in Jesus' teaching. *"For you will be treated as you treat others. The standard you use in judging is the standard by which you will be judged"* (Matthew 7:2, NLT).

When we fail to be a conduit to others of God's love, we end up blocking it from ourselves as well. Jesus said, *"Listen carefully to what I am saying – and be wary of the shrewd advice that tells you how to get ahead in the world on your own. Giving, not getting, is the way. Generosity begets generosity. Stinginess impoverishes"* (Mark 4:24, MSG).

God's discipline as proof of his love

"My child, don't reject the Lord's discipline, and don't be upset when he corrects you. For the Lord corrects those he loves, just as a father corrects a child in whom he delights" (Proverbs 3:11-12, NLT).

"Think about it: Just as a parent disciplines a child, the Lord your God disciplines you for your own good" (Deuteronomy 8:5, NLT).

"My child, don't make light of the Lord's discipline, and don't give up when he corrects you. For the Lord disciplines those he loves, and he punishes each one he accepts as his child. As you endure this divine discipline, remember that God is treating you as his own children. Who ever heard of a child who is never disciplined by its father? If God doesn't discipline you as he does all of his children, it means that you are illegitimate and are not really his children at all . . .

God's discipline is always good for us, so that we might share in his holiness. No discipline is enjoyable while it is happening – it's painful! But afterward there will be a peaceful harvest of right living for those who are trained in this way" (Hebrews 12:5-11, NLT).

Wishing God would love us differently

We naturally tend to equate God's love with giving us what we want and shielding us from pain. In so doing, we reveal our immaturity. Like the child running from discipline, we are asking God for less than his best, less love rather than more.

The fact that he takes us as we are – condemned sinners and enemies of his holy character – and adopts us as his children does not mean that he will leave us in the pathetic state he found us.

Certainly it is love that enables him to take us in that state, but it would not be love to leave us that way. As a good father, he must begin the process of transforming us into something increasingly lovable – for our own good as well as the good of everyone around us.

Transforming us without violating our free will complicates the process, often requiring painful circumstances to shatter our illusions. The steady diet of half-truths we absorb from our culture is designed to keep us enslaved to the current master of this fallen world. Although God gives us glimpses of peace and joy that come with surrender to his will, we find it difficult to override the deceitful lie that such surrender is too costly.

Fortunately, God is patient. He does not force us against our will, but neither does he abandon us to our inferior wishes.

Anyone who has parented a teenager knows the difficulty of managing this tension. Dr. Jay Kesler, a good friend and lifelong example, describes it as trying to land a ten-pound trout on two-pound test line. Exert no pressure, and you will never bring it closer. Exert too much pressure, and you will break the line. Patient, constant adjustments appropriate for this specific ten-pound trout are the ticket.

We, as parents, do our best. God does better. But in our natural state of chronic rebellion, we still don't like the tension of the line.

The next time you are tempted to wish that God would love you differently, think long and hard about who knows more about wise, sacrificial love.

When I realize I have a difference of opinion with God, what is the only logical conclusion I can draw? He's missing something in this equation? I know you can't hear me laughing right now, but the absurdity is hilarious. Even more absurd is that I have made such appeals, hoping that I could help him see some detail I thought he must be overlooking – something that would make *my* case an exception. The realization makes me want to laugh and cry at the same time.

Since God has proven his love through the sacrifice of his own Son, how can we not fully trust the logic of Paul's claim in Romans 8:32? *"Since he did not spare even his own Son but gave him up for us all, won't he also give us everything else?"* (NLT).

This brings us to the midpoint of the Identity part of the Peace Credo. In a capsule:

God's identity: the Creator (and sustainer) of everything.

Your identity: the object (made in his image) of his unfailing love; the recipient of his unfailing peace.

13

My Identity – Child

I am Your loved **child** . . .

You, the Creator of everything, are Sovereign, Providential, and Redemptive.
I am your loved child, redeemed by the blood of Jesus Christ and being transformed daily.
I choose to trust you and your plan before understanding it.
Thank you for your good plan and how you are working it out in my life.
Repenting of all known sin, I choose to live fully forgiven.
I forgive everyone for everything.
I cast every care on you.

"See what great love the Father has lavished on us, that we should be called children of God! And that is what we are!" (1 John 3:1, NIV).

The gift of sonship

Note: I don't mean for "sonship" in this heading to be gender specific, but we don't have a good word for "childship." And I don't want to get into the clumsy habit of sonship/daughtership (another nonword) or his/her, etc. to placate the easily offended. It's hard enough for the grammarian in me to use the plural "they," "them," or "their" for a single person, but I have done it more than once in this book despite my attempts to find better solutions. I pray you will trust my heart in honoring women – without whom none of us would be here. [One of my great regrets in life is that I will never have the privilege of giving birth to a child that God has formed and nurtured inside of me. This everyday miracle is one I view with reverential awe and will NEVER get over. Just thinking of it reduces me to tears.] Women, you have my admiration and deepest respect.

You were not born a child of God. You were born into sin, with a predisposition to rebel against God's authority and make yourself the ruler of your life. I'm not picking on you; it's true of all of us. *". . . sin entered the world through one man, and death through sin, and in this way death came to all people, because all sinned"* (Romans 5:12, NIV).

If you're anything like me, you probably didn't wait until you were two years old to exercise your rebellious will; it just took that long before you could put recognizable words to it – words like "No!" and "Mine!"

The fact that all of us have been made *"in the likeness of God"* (Genesis 5:1, ESV), does not mean that we are all children of God. *"But to all who believed him and accepted him, he gave the right to become children of God"* (John 1:12, NLT). The *"right"* to become a child of God is a gift Jesus has given *"to all who believed and accepted him."*

"So in Christ Jesus you are all children of God through faith" (Galatians 3:26, NIV).

Remember our earlier discussion in Chapter 4 about our spirit and how we define it? This is interesting: *"God's Spirit joins himself to our spirits to declare that we are God's children"* (Romans 8:16, GNT).

We have been chosen

Our ability to believe and accept Jesus – the prerequisite to becoming a child of God – is not a matter of coincidence. *"For he chose us in him before the creation of the world to be holy and blameless in his sight. In love he predestined us for adoption to sonship through Jesus Christ, in accordance with his pleasure and will – to the praise of his glorious grace, which he has freely given us in the One he loves"* (Ephesians 1:4-6, NIV).

But we were not chosen based on our worthiness or self-righteousness. *"God saved you by his grace when you believed. And you can't take credit for this; it is a gift from God. Salvation is not a reward for the good things we have done, so none of us can boast about it"* (Ephesians 2:8-9, NLT).

". . . This message shows that God chooses people according to his own purposes; he calls people, but not according to their good or bad works" (Romans 9:11-12, NLT).

Our inheritance as children of God

"Because you are his sons, God sent the Spirit of his Son into our hearts, the Spirit who calls out, 'Abba, Father.' So you are no longer a slave, but God's child; and since you are his child, God has made you also an heir" (Galatians 4:6-7, NIV).

"And since we are his children, we are his heirs. In fact, together with Christ we are heirs of God's glory. But if we are to share his glory, we must also share his suffering" (Romans 8:17, NLT).

Finally, our inheritance as God's children includes some amazing promises as the foundation for the deep peace Jesus has provided for us.

"*A slave is not a permanent member of the family, but a son is part of the family forever. So if the Son sets you free, you are **truly free***" (John 8:35-36, NLT, emphasis added).

"*He who did not spare his own Son but gave him up for us all, how will he not also with him **graciously give us all things?***" (Romans 8:32, ESV, emphasis added).

"*And **God will generously provide all you need**. Then you will always have everything you need and plenty left over to share with others*" (2 Corinthians 9:8, NLT, emphasis added).

"*Keep your lives free from the love of money and be content with what you have, because **God has said, 'Never will I leave you; never will I forsake you'***" (Hebrews 13:5, NIV, emphasis added).

"*Little children, you are from God and have overcome them [false prophets], for **he who is in you is greater than he who is in the world***" (1 John 4:4, ESV, emphasis added).

"*The thief comes only to steal and kill and destroy; **I have come that they may have life, and have it to the full***" (John 10:10, NIV, emphasis added).

"*Yes, I am the vine; you are the branches. Those who remain in me, and I in them, **will produce much fruit**. For apart from me you can do nothing*" (John 15:5, NLT, emphasis added).

"*Teach these new disciples to obey all the commands I have given you. And be sure of this: **I am***

with you always, even to the end of the age" (Matthew 28:20, NLT, emphasis added).

"*Don't let your hearts be troubled. Trust in God, and trust also in me. There is more than enough room in my Father's home. If this were not so, would I have told you that I am going to prepare a place for you? When everything is ready, I will come and get you, so that **you will always be with me where I am**"* (John 14:1-3, NLT, emphasis added).

And finally, this: ***"Every child of God can defeat the world,*** *and our faith is what gives us this victory"* (1 John 5:4, CEV, emphasis added).

14

My Identity – Redeemed

I am Your loved child, **redeemed by the blood of Jesus Christ . . .**

You, the Creator of everything, are Sovereign, Providential, and Redemptive.
I am your loved child, redeemed by the blood of Jesus Christ and being transformed daily.
I choose to trust you and your plan before understanding it.
Thank you for your good plan and how you are working it out in my life.
Repenting of all known sin, I choose to live fully forgiven.
I forgive everyone for everything.
I cast every care on you.

". . . you are in Christ Jesus, who became to us . . . redemption [providing our ransom from the penalty for sin]" (1 Corinthians 1:30, AMP).

Bought back

To be redeemed is to be bought back. When someone pawns a possession, she sells her right of ownership to it. She can, however, buy back the object by paying an agreed-upon redemption price. This reinstates her ownership.

The same concept applies to the ownership of human beings. A free man is deemed to own himself. But if by his own choice (indentured servitude) or by force (slavery) he is bought by someone, he no longer owns himself. To become free again, his obligation to his owner must be paid in full. That is his redemption price.

Since the Fall, we are all slaves to sin. *"When Adam sinned, sin entered the world. Adam's sin brought death, so death spread to everyone, for everyone sinned"* (Romans 5:12, NLT).

Although we think we are in control of our own lives, we are under the pervasive influence of Satan, powerless to defeat his deceptions. In Romans 6:19, Paul says, *"Because of the weakness of your human nature, I am using the illustration of slavery to help you understand all this. Previously, you let yourselves be slaves to impurity and lawlessness, which led ever deeper into sin"* (NLT).

Peter says simply, *"For you are a slave to whatever controls you"* (2 Peter 2:19, NLT). This slavery to sin continues unabated until God steps in.

Paul speaks of the great contrast: *"Once you were alienated from God and were enemies in your minds because of your evil behavior. But now he has reconciled you by Christ's physical body through death to present you holy in his sight, without blemish and free from accusation"* (Colossians 1:21-22, NIV).

We are bought back by the payment of our redemption price – a price higher than any mere human could pay.

Peter describes it this way: *"For you know that God paid a ransom to [redeem] you from the empty life you inherited from your ancestors. And it was not paid with mere gold or silver, which lose their value. It was the precious blood of Christ, the sinless, spotless Lamb of God"* (1 Peter 1:18-19, NLT).

The blood of Jesus Christ

Jesus said, *"This is my blood, which confirms the covenant between God and his people. It is poured out as a sacrifice to forgive the sins of many"* (Matthew 26:28, NLT).

Hebrews 9:16-22 further underscores the significance of Jesus' blood in our redemption. *"For where a will is involved, the death of the one who made it must be established. 17 For a will takes effect only at death, since it is not in force as long as the one who made it is alive. 18 Therefore not even the first covenant was inaugurated without blood. 19 For when every commandment of the law had been declared by Moses to all the people, he took the blood of calves and goats, with water and scarlet wool and hyssop, and sprinkled both the book itself and all the people, 20 saying, 'This is the blood of the covenant that God commanded for you.' 21 And in the same way he sprinkled with the blood both the tent and all the vessels used in worship. 22 Indeed, under the law almost everything is purified with blood, and **without the shedding of blood there is no forgiveness of sins"*** (ESV, emphasis added).

This redemption is at the heart of God's new covenant with us. It is also the doorway into our inheritance in Christ.

In Chapter 9 we briefly discussed the sovereign covenants God has made with us. In Chapter 13 we quoted many Scriptures that describe our inheritance as sons and daughters of God by faith through grace. This next passage ties together the **new covenant** and our **inheritance** by **redemption** through the **sacrificial death of Christ.**

*"Therefore he is the mediator of a **new covenant**, so that those who are called may receive the promised **eternal inheritance**, since a death has occurred that **redeems** them from the transgressions committed under the first covenant ... He [Christ] has appeared once for all at the end of the ages to put away sin by the **sacrifice** of himself. And just as it is appointed for man to die once, and after that comes judgment, so Christ, having been offered once to bear the sins of many, will appear a second time, not to deal with sin but **to save** those who are eagerly waiting for him"* (Hebrews 9:15, 26-28, ESV, emphasis added).

Remember that God had warned Adam in the Garden, *"You may freely eat the fruit of every tree in the garden – except the tree of the knowledge of good and evil. If you eat its fruit, you are sure to die"* (Genesis 2:16-17, NLT). How do we reconcile the fact that he ate the fruit and continued to live?

We might say that God didn't specify that he would die immediately – just that he would die. And in due time he did. But prior to that, he died in a more important way. His spirit – the most important part of him – died from contamination by sin.

Paul clarifies this when he declares good news for us. *"You were dead because of your sins and because your sinful nature was not yet cut away. Then God made you alive with Christ, for he forgave all our sins. He canceled the record of the charges against us and took it away by nailing it to the cross. In this way, he disarmed the spiritual rulers and authorities. He shamed them publicly by his victory over them on the cross"* (Colossians 2:13-15, NLT).

Notice that Paul says God *"disarmed the spiritual rulers and authorities."* What is he talking about? We don't generally think of Satan and his followers as spiritual rulers and authorities, but that is their role on this fallen planet.

I believe they use us as evidence in their attempt to show the angelic realm that God was unjust in sentencing them – by proving that we, like them, will rebel against God if we have the opportunity.

They take God's good law, mislead and tempt us to break it, and then condemn us for our failure. But God has disarmed them – taken away the power of their accusations – when he put our guilt on Jesus, nailing it to the cross.

This is what it means to be redeemed by the blood of Jesus Christ. Our former master is disarmed. The redemption price is paid in full. *"I have been crucified with Christ and I no longer live, but Christ lives in me. The life I now live in the body, I live by faith in the Son of God, who loved me and gave himself for me"* (Galatians 2:20, NIV). By faith we have access into a new life now – *"in the body"* – and eternal life when God takes us home.

15

My Identity – Being transformed daily

I am Your loved child, redeemed by the blood of Jesus Christ and **being transformed daily.**

> You, the Creator of everything, are Sovereign, Providential, and Redemptive.
> **I am your loved child, redeemed by the blood of Jesus Christ and being transformed daily.**
> I choose to trust you and your plan before understanding it.
> Thank you for your good plan and how you are working it out in my life.
> Repenting of all known sin, I choose to live fully forgiven.
> I forgive everyone for everything.
> I cast every care on you.

We are being transformed. *"And we all, with unveiled face, beholding the glory of the Lord, are **being transformed** into the same image from one degree of glory to another. For this comes from the Lord who is the Spirit"* (2 Corinthians 3:18, ESV, emphasis added).

Notice how the Peace Credo's second line (bold above) presents its three concepts in the same order as this next passage: loved child, redeemed, and transformed. *"For those God foreknew* **[loved children]** *he also predestined to be conformed to the image of his Son, that he might be the firstborn among many brothers and sisters. And those he predestined, he also called; those he called, he also justified*

[redeemed]; *those he justified, he also glorified"* **[transformed]** (Romans 8:29-30, NIV).

Transformation is a buzzword in our culture. What does it mean?

Transformed = born again and sanctified
*"Jesus replied, 'I tell you the truth, unless you are **born again,** you cannot see the Kingdom of God'"* (John 3:3, NLT, emphasis added).

*". . . It is by his great mercy that we have been **born again,** because God raised Jesus Christ from the dead. Now we live with great expectation"* (1 Peter 1:3, NLT, emphasis added).

". . . you are in Christ Jesus, who became to us . . . ***sanctification** [making us holy and setting us apart for God]"* (1 Corinthians 1:30, AMP, emphasis added).

One of Webster's definitions of "transform" is "to change in character or condition." Both of these changes – character and condition – happen when we are redeemed by the blood of Christ.

Changed condition
Our condition changes immediately: we go from condemned to pardoned, from slaves of sin to children of God, from a hopeless future to a joy-filled eternity with our savior. *"Therefore, if anyone is in Christ, the new creation has come: The old has gone, the new is here!"* (2 Corinthians 5:17, NIV).

Changing character
Our character, on the other hand, changes incrementally. It's the day-by-day process of sanctification as the Holy Spirit and the Word work

together to bring us to spiritual maturity. *"God has chosen you from the beginning for salvation through the **sanctifying work of the Spirit** [that sets you apart for God's purpose] and by your faith in the truth [of God's word **that leads you to spiritual maturity**]"* (2 Thessalonians 2:13, AMP, emphasis added). This progressively changes our outlook, our motivation, our attitude, and our behavior.

So, our condition changes immediately and permanently, but our character transformation is always a work in progress. An ongoing internal war between our old nature (character) and our new one is typically two steps forward and one step back.

The frustrating backward steps occur whenever we climb back onto the throne of our life, asserting our own kingship. It isn't always an overt act of rebellion: it's just giving in to our self-centered focus.

Our default is to choose control and comfort over submission to God's better plan that we don't yet trust. We forget that we're straining to see the future through blindfolds while he has full access to it as though it were this very moment.

As born-again believers, we usually exercise faith when we stop and think carefully. In our best moments we choose to trust God's better plan for us even before we see it clearly and understand it. *"Trust in the Lord with all your heart; do not depend on your own understanding. Seek his will in all you do, and he will show you which path to take"* (Proverbs 3:5-6, NLT).

But then ten minutes later, that conscious choice is replaced by the demands of the moment, and we revert to our default – the habit of self-reliance and trusting our own understanding. The remedy? *"Do not conform to the pattern of this world, but be **transformed** by the renewing of your mind"* (Romans 12:2, NIV, emphasis added).

God takes our transformation seriously, never doubting its ultimate completion. And he asks us to have the same confidence – not because we can pull it off, but because he, the great "I AM," is the Prime Mover. *"Being confident of this, that he who began a good work in you will carry it on to completion until the day of Christ Jesus"* (Philippians 1:6, NIV).

Conflicts continue
Until the process is complete, most of our conflicts are related to four classes of issues: identity (who God is and who we are), trust, attitude, and obedience.

These are the components of the Peace Credo, the foundational areas where the enemy works in the dark to conform us to *"the pattern of this world"* without our conscious awareness. He quietly builds a practical "working theology" out of clever rationalizations that appeal to our old character. Consider these examples.

- Go ahead; everybody does it.
- You can't afford to trust God; he's got bigger fish to fry.
- It's okay as long as you get away with it.
- What's done in Vegas stays in Vegas.
- Make sure you get what's coming to you; no one else cares.
- No problem: no one will ever know.

- Don't go out of your way for them; they wouldn't do it for you.
- Your personal life is your own private business.
- How can it be wrong if it feels so right?
- Go ahead; doesn't God want you to be happy?

When these flawed assumptions fuel our autopilot, it's not a good thing. But the 40-second Peace Credo brings them into view, enabling us to see the flaws and shine the appropriate Scriptures on them.

Transformation agents: the Spirit and the Word
The Spirit, in conjunction with God's word, is working to transform us, to renew our minds. But he doesn't force his way in; he patiently waits for our cooperation in the process.

This is why memorizing and frequently repeating the Peace Credo is so important: it's like an instant reboot. This flash inspection of our basic programming enables us to see our software conflicts and replace the corrupted code, *"the pattern of this world,"* with the truth of God's word.

Seven pillars
Of the Peace Credo's seven statements, the first two deal with identity; the third with trust; the fourth with attitude, and the last three with practical obedience. All of these are in line with God's character and his Great Command to love him first and love our neighbor as ourselves. The seven statements work together, allowing God's peace to reign in our hearts, a preemptive strike against fear and anxiety.

Results

Look at the results of the transformation God is producing in us: renewed thoughts and attitudes, new nature, righteous and holy.

"Let the Spirit renew your thoughts and attitudes. Put on your new nature, created to be like God – truly righteous and holy" (Ephesians 4:23-24, NLT).

And it doesn't stop there. He gives us knowledge of the paths of life (wisdom) and fills us with joy. *"You have made known to me the paths of life; you will fill me with joy in your presence"* (Acts 2:28, NIV).

16

Choosing to Trust

I choose to **trust** you . . .

You, the Creator of everything, are Sovereign, Providential, and Redemptive.
I am your loved child, redeemed by the blood of Jesus Christ and being transformed daily.
I choose to trust you and your plan before understanding it.
Thank you for your good plan and how you are working it out in my life.
Repenting of all known sin, I choose to live fully forgiven.
I forgive everyone for everything.
I cast every care on you.

"A man is a fool to trust himself! But those who use God's wisdom are safe" (Proverbs 28:26, TLB).

If we have even the slightest idea of who God really is – his power and attributes – the question of whether to trust him would never come up.

Unfortunately, Satan deceives us on many fronts, beginning with distorting God's nature and his intentions with us.

This dates back to Eden, where Satan showed his own fatal flaw. When he convinced Eve that God was holding out on her, it revealed his own belief that God was holding out on him. He longed for God's power and position and was denied it.

Why was he denied? Only God himself can occupy that position because only God himself cannot be tempted by sin.

Choose

". . . Choose this day whom you will serve . . ." (Joshua 24:15, ESV). Before we dig deeper into the crucial issue of trust, I want to explore this word, *"choose."*

We've already discussed how God has honored us with free will, giving us the power to choose to love him or to rebel. We know that choosing is an act of our will. Although it involves feeling, it is much more than mere emotion.

We make some choices after deliberate analysis and logical conclusions. We make many others, however, through conscious and subconscious intuition. As acknowledged in Chapters 4 and 5, we base these choices on assumption clusters and beliefs that are often a jumble of facts, errors, and feelings.

But now I want to touch on a different aspect of choosing. Our choices – even the best ones – are rarely permanent. Just think of your last round of New Year resolutions. Or maybe you didn't even make any because you've seen so many in the past fizzle after a few weeks – or even a few days. It's discouraging to see resolve fade so soon, but this doesn't make you a failure; it makes you human.

In light of this, we start the Peace Credo's third line with the words "I choose." You are stating your intention. You know that at some point you will fail to follow through perfectly, and your trust will crumble. Maybe you give in to a feeling or a weakness or a deception. What do you do then? Simply choose again.

You start all over by declaring your renewed intent to trust. You make a fresh choice. The right one.

Again. As many times as it takes. Until you leave the earth for a sinless eternity with your savior.

In the meantime, God knows all about it and is there to help. *"The Spirit helps us with our weakness. We do not know how to pray as we should. But the Spirit himself speaks to God for us, even begs God for us with deep feelings that words cannot explain"* (Romans 8:26, NCV).

"In God we trust" – not self

God speaks through Isaiah to give us a compelling reason for trusting him over ourselves: *"Just as the heavens are higher than the earth, my thoughts and my ways are higher than yours. That's how it is with my words. They don't return to me without doing everything I send them to do"* (Isaiah 55:9, 11, CEV).

Isaiah responded by choosing to trust God. This is what he experienced: *"You will keep in perfect peace all who trust in you, all whose thoughts are fixed on you!"* (Isaiah 26:3, NLT).

Nearly 700 years before God described the power of his word to the prophet Isaiah, he confirmed his ever-present help by telling Joshua, *"I've commanded you to be strong and brave. Don't ever be afraid or discouraged! I am the Lord your God, and I will be there to help you wherever you go"* (Joshua 1:9, CEV).

About 140 years before Isaiah's declaration, King David described his daily choice this way. *"Each morning let me learn more about your love **because I trust you.** I come to you in prayer asking for your guidance"* (Psalm 143:8, CEV, emphasis added). The Lord promises, *"I will guide you along the best* *pathway for your life. I will advise you and watch over you"* (Psalm 32:8, NLT).

Asking for and trusting in God's guidance is the wisest choice we can make. David trusted God implicitly for his unseen future. *"But I am trusting you, O Lord, saying, 'You are my God!' My future is in your hands"* (Psalm 31:14-15, NLT).

Trusting God leads to a quality of life nothing else can match. *"[The Lord]* **takes pleasure in** *those who honor him, in* **those who trust in his constant love"** (Psalm 147:11, GNT, emphasis added).

Because of his trust in God's love, David went on to compare himself to a flourishing olive tree.

Did you know that some olive trees living today in the City of David (Jerusalem) were alive when Jesus walked there? One in Bethlehem, the al Badawi tree, is believed by some researchers to be the oldest living tree in the world, estimated at 4,000 to 5,000 years old. That gives new meaning to this Psalm from David: *"But I am like an olive tree flourishing in the house of God;* **I trust in God's unfailing love** *for ever and ever"* (Psalm 52:8, NIV, emphasis added).

From a lifetime of experience, David, who knew well his own weaknesses, knew that God was the only one worthy of his trust. And not only his trust, but his people's trust. That's why he pleaded with them to, *"Trust in him at all times, you people; pour out your hearts to him, for God is our refuge"* (Psalm 62:8, NIV).

Bottom line: I simply rely on God's demonstrated trustworthiness because of everything in the identity statements that comprise lines one and two of the

Peace Credo. He, the Creator of everything, is sovereign, providential, and redemptive – every base is covered. And I am his loved child, proven by the extreme sacrifice he made to redeem and adopt me. If that combination doesn't scream trustworthy, it can only be because we are hard of hearing.

The more frequently and completely I choose to trust, the greater confidence I develop in the moral certainty of God's faithfulness. Peace relies on this.

17

Trusting God's Plan

I choose to trust you and your plan . . .

You, the Creator of everything, are Sovereign, Providential, and Redemptive.
I am your loved child, redeemed by the blood of Jesus Christ and being transformed daily.
I choose to trust you and your plan before understanding it.
Thank you for your good plan and how you are working it out in my life.
Repenting of all known sin, I choose to live fully forgiven.
I forgive everyone for everything.
I cast every care on you.

Trusting is a challenge

Trusting the invisible God has always been a challenge. Trusting the visible Jesus was not always easy, either, because he radically challenges the religious status quo. In John 6, Jesus describes himself as the living bread, saying that *"unless you eat the flesh of the Son of Man and drink his blood, you have no life in you"* (verse 53, ESV). And *"whoever feeds on this bread will live forever"* (verse 58).

He lost a lot of disciples that day.

Think about this conversation that followed: *"So Jesus said to the twelve, 'Do you want to go away as well?' Simon Peter answered him, 'Lord, to whom shall we go? You have the words of eternal life, and we have believed, and have come to know, that you are the Holy One of God'"* (verses 67-69). It's a difficult time, but Peter chooses to trust.

This is the same Peter, who in a moment of fear and weakness a short time later, denies he even knows Jesus. But then later still – come on, you knew it was coming – he again **chooses** to trust. In spite of past failures, he chooses to trust again. And God honors Peter's renewed choice to trust.

Learning to trust again

In recognition of our own tendency to falter in times of fear and weakness, Maria and I recorded "Learning to Trust Again" in 1993. During our performances onstage, some people in our audiences may have thought we were granted a charmed life.

We knew better, and we openly talked about the dark times we experienced, including the loss of a twin and the pain of depression. But people have a way of thinking their own difficulties are "more real" than those of others.

In this song, we hoped to communicate that we all suffer and that trust is a dynamic choice, that it needs to be chosen and acknowledged over and over again. As one of our mentors used to say, "it's committing everything I know about myself to everything I know about God." And that changes every day.

Learning to Trust Again

Standing here in front of you, wondering what to say,
Wishing that you could read my mind
And know my thoughts today.
We've all been through such pain and loss,
We thought we could not bear,
Misunderstood and so alone, no feelings left but fear.

But now we're learning to trust again in a deeper kind of way,

Learning to trust again the process of today.
Knowing that He will finish well what He's begun in me,
That everything fits in the end, I'm learning to trust Him again.

In all the scenes of memories past,
Through all the tears I've shed,
I see His rainbow standing fast. It is just as He said.
Give up your fear, my precious child, if you belong to me,
Though you may not yet understand, one day you'll clearly see.

And so we're learning to trust again in a deeper kind of way,
Learning to trust again the process of today.
Knowing that He will finish well what He's begun in me,
That everything fits in the end, I'm learning to trust Him again.

Lyrics and music by Steve Gardner © 1993 Aslan Family Music/ASCAP

It ain't the cross

Regardless of the suffering God has allowed in your life, it can't compare to what Jesus experienced for us.

One of our good friends suffering with diabetes, kidney failure, and frequent, long rounds of dialysis, has a great response when we ask how he is doing. Knowing that we're not just asking out of courtesy but that we really want to hear what he's feeling, he describes his latest symptoms and reactions to treatment. And then he always follows with, "But it ain't the cross." In other words, the ultimate sacrifice of Jesus gives him courage to bear up under his circumstances, courage to trust again.

Think about the depth of trust and the courage the disciples showed after Jesus, their leader and Lord, was crucified. Thomas may have been the last to recognize the risen Jesus, but he certainly wasn't the only one with doubts and fears. *"On the evening of that day, the first day of the week,* ***the doors being*** *locked where the disciples were for fear of the Jews, Jesus came and stood among them and said to them, 'Peace be with you'"* (John 20:19, ESV, emphasis added). They were all fearful, and they all had to learn to trust again.

After the Holy Spirit was given to them, they proclaimed God's truth with great power. They also endured unbelievable hardships and barbaric deaths. They chose to trust again over and over in their zeal to turn the world upside down with what they had witnessed firsthand. They knew that Jesus was *"the way, and the truth, and the life"* (John 14:6, ESV). They also had confidence that God was working out his plan in his own time and way.

God's plan

"'For I know the plans I have for you,' declares the Lord, 'plans to prosper you and not to harm you, plans to give you hope and a future'" (Jeremiah 29:11, NIV). This promise is not an insurance policy against disaster in this life. God frequently rewards his children with the blessing of prosperity, but it isn't always financial. Thank God that it isn't!

Financial wealth is no guarantee of happiness, and it is just the opposite when we let it come before God in our priorities. But when we put him first, he rewards us with *"a hope and future."* The hope includes his unfailing peace, and the future is one that will not rust or fade and can never be taken from us.

The plan, however, never unfolds as we expect or even as we hope and pray. Sovereign God, from his unique vantage point, is working out a plan far too complex for us to comprehend. That's what God was telling Isaiah when he said, *"Just as the heavens are higher than the earth, my thoughts and my ways are higher than yours."*

We get the broad strokes – enough to assure us of the big picture – but we can't begin to understand how he *"works all things together for good,"* especially the painful ones we would never choose.

God's plan versus mine

Every day I am choosing again to trust God and his plan. Of course I have my own plans, and they seem really good to me. I think God should like them. And I'd like him to enforce them. I even think he likes me to share them with him – for multiple reasons, but certainly not to enlighten him. I think he desires me to pour out my heart to him in all candor.

And then he desires me to say, "But as much as I like my plan, I desperately want you to trump it. I KNOW your plan is far superior. I vote for yours. Please guide me."

18

Understanding

I choose to trust you and your plan before **understanding** it.

You, the Creator of everything, are Sovereign, Providential, and Redemptive.
I am your loved child, redeemed by the blood of Jesus Christ and being transformed daily.
I choose to trust you and your plan before understanding it.
Thank you for your good plan and how you are working it out in my life.
Repenting of all known sin, I choose to live fully forgiven.
I forgive everyone for everything.
I cast every care on you.

"Oh, how great are God's riches and wisdom and knowledge! How impossible it is for us to understand his decisions and his ways!" (Romans 11:33, NLT).

Okay, that's nice. Great thought there, Paul. And I see you're echoing Isaiah with the idea that God's thoughts and ways are impossibly higher than ours. I've been quoting him too. Next?

"The Lord directs our steps, so why try to understand everything along the way?" Proverbs 20:24, (NLT).

But I WANT (Can you hear the whine?) to understand. I NEED to understand. Otherwise, how can I decide to say yes and go all in? Wait, did I just say that? Must have been a Freudian slip, which I think means saying the truth when I didn't really mean to.

Just think of the implications. I need to understand in order to cooperate with the Creator of the universe on what he's directing for my benefit?

And if I don't understand, I should do what? Hold out for my idea that I do understand?

Sure, that makes sense. Except that I have no insight into the future. My predictive skills leave a lot to be desired. Nor do I have much control over the present – virtually none over the decisions of others or the occurrence of global events, natural disasters, or even whether my health will continue for another month, week, or day.

The value of my understanding

Maybe I don't understand as much as I think I do. And maybe a lot of what I understand is better defined as misunderstanding. But since it occurs in *my* head, I tend to give it credibility and prefer it over trusting the One who really does understand. And who happens to be Sovereign, Providential, and Redemptive.

Relying on my understanding over his is a better definition of insanity than the one we frequently hear: doing the same thing over and over and expecting a different result. Unfortunately, the two definitions probably coincide most of the time.

"Trust in the Lord with all your heart; do not depend on your own understanding" (Proverbs 3:5, NLT). Am I sensing a theme here? I'm pretty sure God is not opposed to understanding. In fact, he's the one who gives it – even to Solomon, the guy who wrote Proverbs 3:5 that we just quoted. *"God gave Solomon*

very great wisdom and understanding, and knowledge as vast as the sands of the seashore" (1 Kings 4:29, NLT).

As we look at the "before understanding it" theme of the Peace Credo, realize that we're not bashing understanding. But we do want to examine how it can get twisted and used by the enemy. First, let's check out some verses in praise of understanding.

- *"God gave these four young men an unusual aptitude for understanding every aspect of literature and wisdom"* (Daniel 1:17, NLT).
- *"For the Lord grants wisdom! From his mouth come knowledge and understanding"* (Proverbs 2:6, NLT).
- *"Joyful is the person who finds wisdom, the one who gains understanding"* (Proverbs 3:13, NLT).
- *"He has showered his kindness on us, along with all wisdom and understanding"* (Ephesians 1:8, NLT).
- *"And we know that the Son of God has come, and he has given us understanding so that we can know the true God"* (1 John 5:20, NLT).
- *"I pray that your love will overflow more and more, and that you will keep on growing in knowledge and understanding"* (Philippians 1:9, NLT).
- *"And may the Lord give you wisdom and understanding"* (1 Chronicles 22:12, NLT).
- *"And so, God willing, we will move forward to further understanding"* (Hebrews 6:3, NLT).

In light of all these verses proclaiming the value of understanding – and they are only a sampling of a much larger list – why does the Peace Credo seem to downplay understanding? See if you catch some clues from these additional verses.

Pseudo-understanding

"Fools have no interest in understanding; they only want to air their own opinions" (Proverbs 18:2, NLT). This verse hints at the pervasive problem of pseudo-understanding. Fools do not often admit that they have no interest in understanding. Instead, they insist that they do understand. When they say, "I don't understand you" what they really mean is "I disagree with you." Often they haven't really heard and considered what you have to say because they are closed to anything other than their own opinion.

Here's the hard part: we recognize this pattern in others, but we don't see it in ourselves. And yet that is what we do with God when we're pushing our own agenda.

"Let those with understanding receive guidance" (Proverbs 1:5, NLT). We tend to think that once we understand, we don't really need guidance – we've already got it covered, thank you very much. However, *really* understanding reveals our desperate need for guidance.

Our desire to be self-sufficient is healthy when it comes to being responsible, but it is very unhealthy when it implies that we can take care of ourselves without God's direction. *"The wise man is glad to be instructed, but a self-sufficient fool falls flat on his face"* (Proverbs 10:8, TLB).

We need the balance Paul found in 2 Corinthians 3:5, *"Not that we are sufficient in ourselves to claim anything as coming from us, but our sufficiency is from God."*

You don't have to understand God's plans to receive his guidance. Simply understanding that both his power and character exceed yours should be enough to prefer his guidance over your own strategy.

I still want to understand, but I've learned that trust must precede understanding. Faith is about what cannot yet be seen. God has chosen faith to be the currency of the believer because it is not dependent on intellect – not limited to the educated elite.

I trust first and then learn to understand. If I demand to understand first, *I make myself God's judge* – arrogantly rebellious.

The fear of the Lord

"And the Spirit of the Lord will rest on him — the Spirit of wisdom and understanding, the Spirit of counsel and might, the Spirit of knowledge and the fear of the Lord" (Isaiah 11:2, NLT). Notice how all of these positive attributes – wisdom, understanding, counsel, might, and knowledge – culminate in *"the fear of the Lord."* What does that term mean?

A common answer, and I think a good one, is that *"the fear of the Lord"* means to hate evil. *"To fear the Lord is to hate evil. I hate pride, arrogance, evil behavior, and twisted speech"* (Proverbs 8:13, GW).

We reason that if God is God and we are his created subjects, we would do well to love what he loves and hate what he hates. That could also be called common sense. But why should it conjure up a sense of fear? Why *"the 'fear' of the Lord"*?

Since we have so many commands from God (and his angels speaking for him) *not* to fear, we're a little uncomfortable using the word "fear" to describe a healthy attitude toward him. We usually rely on some other descriptor like "reverential awe" to explain it.

The real meaning of "awe"

But even the word "awe" has lost much of its edge in our modern culture. The most accurate synonyms for its original meaning are "dread" and "terror." Webster now defines "awe" this way: "an emotion variously combining dread, veneration, and wonder that is inspired by authority or by the sacred or sublime."

I am as guilty as anyone of cheapening the word "awesome" by easily applying it to everything from a touchdown pass to a slice of pizza. That's unfortunate, because we would be better off reserving it for its true meaning: dread, veneration, and wonder in response to God's power – *"the fear of the Lord."*

You're familiar with the Bible story about Jesus and the disciples in a boat during a storm. What you may not have noticed is the curious ending of the story and how abruptly it concludes the chapter. Check this out. *"On that day, when evening had come, he [Jesus] said to them, 'Let us go across to the other side.' [36]And leaving the crowd, they took him with them in the boat . . . [37]And a great windstorm arose, and the waves were breaking into the boat, so that the boat was already filling. [38]But he was in the stern, asleep on the cushion.*

And they woke him and said to him, 'Teacher, do you not care that we are perishing?' ³⁹*And he awoke and rebuked the wind and said to the sea, 'Peace! Be still!' And the wind ceased, and there was a great calm.* ⁴⁰*He said to them, 'Why are you so afraid? Have you still no faith?'"*

Now note this last sentence: ⁴¹*"And they were filled with **great fear** and said to one another, **'Who then is this, that even the wind and the sea obey him?'"*** (Mark 4:35-41, ESV, emphasis added). Earlier, when the storm was raging and the boat was filling with water, the disciples must have been afraid – at least afraid enough to awaken Jesus. But nothing is said about their fear. Now that the storm is history, the threat has been removed, and the danger is over, they are *"filled with great fear."*

Suddenly realizing the awesome power of the one in the boat with them, an inexplicable *"fear of the Lord"* overtakes them. This is not a moment when they are saying to each other, "Wasn't that interesting?"

Chills and hair standing on end are probably no exaggeration. I doubt that our imaginations can even begin to capture the dread, terror, and wonder of their *"great fear."* This is the creature coming face to face with the creator and realizing the overwhelming power differential. I'm afraid this scene is one where you have to have been there to have more than a vague clue of its visceral impact.

19

Trust Before Understanding

I choose to trust you and your plan **before understanding** it.

You, the Creator of everything, are Sovereign, Providential, and Redemptive.
I am your loved child, redeemed by the blood of Jesus Christ and being transformed daily.
I choose to trust you and your plan before understanding it.
Thank you for your good plan and how you are working it out in my life.
Repenting of all known sin, I choose to live fully forgiven.
I forgive everyone for everything.
I cast every care on you.

Let me try to put *"the fear of the Lord"* into further perspective with a story from my childhood – one that remains vivid in my memory despite the fact that I have forgotten most of the others.

Not living near railroad tracks, I had limited exposure to trains. But I had a lot of fascination with them because of their size and power.

At age eleven or twelve I spent a week at a camp near Grand Junction, MI. An active railroad was a short walk away. As the week went by, I watched several trains pass at high speed. A thought struck me. The engines and cars extend out beyond the tracks by a little bit, but not by much – maybe a couple feet on each side. That means I should be able to stand pretty close to the tracks when one passes and still be safe.

I decided that ten feet out from the rails should be a safe distance, allowing a closeup look without being in any real danger. A friend and I walked to the tracks and waited for the next train. We felt the rails to see whether a train was approaching from somewhere beyond our sight. I have no idea whether that really works, but we had seen Tonto or somebody in a western do it and it seemed like a smart thing to do. I think we heard the train in the distance before we felt anything. Tonto was probably more experienced.

I measured out three long paces, about ten feet, from the rails. My brain told me it should be a safe distance, but my friend wanted a little more margin. He stepped back a few more yards. I gave it another two feet.

Excitement mounted as the massive locomotive sped toward us. My heart started racing, and I was torn between the desire to be brave and the urge to run. I held my ground.

When the engines were about 100 yards away – more or less a city block – I could feel the pressure to retreat mounting. As they grew closer, I swear I could feel a different kind of pressure, the air pressure being pushed out ahead of the speeding train. The sound, growing in pitch and volume, was overpowering – even before the whistle blew.

Was I afraid? Not exactly.

I was terrified. I found myself involuntarily backing up, overwhelmed with dread and terror at the sheer power of this monster bearing down on me. By the time the engines crossed my location, I was probably thirty feet away from the tracks. And even that seemed way too close for comfort.

Was I terrified because the train was evil? Of course not. It was designed to be a benefit. Then why was I afraid? It has something to do with lack of control, but it's more than that. The train had the power to totally undo me, and that kind of power is fearsome. It goes beyond logic, generating a raw emotion that is indescribable. THAT is awe. I am not Superman. I was not made to stand up to a speeding locomotive.

It's like that between us and God except on an infinitely greater scale. Remember when Moses wanted to see God? God acknowledges the massive power differential between himself and humanity when he says, *"'I will make all my goodness pass before you, and I will call out my name, Yahweh, before you.. ... But you may not look directly at my face, for no one may see me and live.' The Lord continued, 'Look, stand near me on this rock. As my glorious presence passes by, I will hide you in the crevice of the rock and cover you with my hand until I have passed by. Then I will remove my hand and let you see me from behind. But my face will not be seen'"* (Exodus 33:19-23, NLT).

Here is how I think of it. *"The Lord takes pleasure in those who fear him, in those who hope in his steadfast love"* (Psalm 147:11, ESV). This makes a lot of sense, but it still doesn't seem to answer why the word *"fear"* is used. We generally think of hope as being one of fear's opposites, a positive replacement for fear. I think the *"fear"* relates to a healthy realization that God has both the power and the right to judge and condemn us. We fear his judgment – as we should – but we *"hope in his steadfast love,"* hoping that he will find a way to forgive and pardon us.

What does Jesus say?
Bottom line? Here is what Jesus says about fearing God. *"Don't be afraid of those who want to kill your body; they cannot touch your soul. Fear only God, who can destroy both soul and body in hell.* 29 *What is the price of two sparrows — one copper coin? But not a single sparrow can fall to the ground without your Father knowing it.* 30 *And the very hairs on your head are all numbered.* 31 *So don't be afraid; you are more valuable to God than a whole flock of sparrows"* (Matthew 10:28-31, NLT). Jesus says to fear God because he is the ultimate power. And then he says, but don't be afraid, because the ultimate power loves you; you are valuable to him!

The *"fear of the Lord"* sets it all up
Back to the point we introduced in the last chapter: all these positive attributes – wisdom, understanding, counsel, might, and knowledge – go hand in hand with *"the fear of the Lord."* Without *"the fear of the Lord"* to set their context and boundaries, these positive attributes are unreliable as guides.

"The fear of the Lord is the beginning of wisdom; all those who practice it have a good understanding" (Psalm 111:10, ESV). A *"good understanding"* is what we want, but a lack of godly priorities leads to pseudo-understanding, like the fool who is wise in his own eyes. *"Do you see a man who is wise in his own eyes?*

There is more hope for a fool than for him" (Proverbs 26:12, ESV).

We want wisdom and understanding that surpass our own. We want them to have the enduring quality of truth, of alignment with the will of the Creator of the universe.

Isaiah testifies, *"The Sovereign Lord has given me his words of wisdom, so that I know how to comfort the weary. Morning by morning he wakens me and opens my understanding to his will"* (Isaiah 50:4, NLT). This is almighty God giving wisdom to a willing subject – one who trusts God's perspective over his own.

"Then he [an angel] said, 'Don't be afraid, Daniel. Since the first day you began to pray for understanding and to humble yourself before your God, your request has been heard in heaven. I have come in answer to your prayer'" (Daniel 10:12, NLT).

What an amazing message! Daniel's prayer heard in heaven. Daniel's attitude seen in heaven. God dispatching an agent in response (The rest of the angel's story is remarkable!).

Do you see the operative connection? *". . . since the first day you began to* **pray for understanding** *and to* **humble yourself before your God.***"* It wasn't about the understanding Daniel already possessed: it was about his humility to seek God's understanding over his own, his desire to gain God's perspective.

Trust precedes understanding

Of course we want understanding, but humbling ourselves before God is a precondition. The attitude cannot be "When I understand, I will submit." I must submit first, and understanding follows. That's what it means to trust.

That's why the Bible says in four places – Habakkuk 2:4, Romans 1:17, Galatians 3:11, and Hebrews 10:38 – *"The just shall live by faith."* Not by sight, but by faith. Not by understanding, but by trust that precedes understanding.

That's why the writer of Hebrews urges, *". . . Let us go on instead and become mature in our understanding."* (Hebrews 6:1, NLT). And Paul pleads, *"May the Lord lead your hearts into a full understanding and expression of the love of God and the patient endurance that comes from Christ"* (2 Thessalonians 3:5, NLT).

We each have to settle for ourselves this chicken-and-egg issue of what comes first, understanding or trust. Just like I couldn't stand firm and hold my ground against the train, *"No human wisdom or understanding or plan can stand against the Lord"* (Proverbs 21:30, NLT).

Hear this clear warning from Jesus: *"So pay attention to how you hear. To those who listen to my teaching, more understanding will be given. But for those who are not listening, even what they **think** they understand will be taken away from them"* (Luke 8:18, NLT, emphasis added).

Those who are not listening may value understanding and *think* they understand, but they, like the fool in Proverbs 18:2, are not listening to obey: they are listening only to evaluate, to make themselves God's judge. *"They only want to air their own opinions."*

Read Proverbs 3:5 (NLT) again, this time with two key words highlighted: *"Trust in the Lord with all your heart; do not depend on **your own** understanding."* This is the principle of trust and obedience before understanding – the whole point.

And it is further underscored in these last two proverbs: *"I will pursue your commands, for you expand my understanding" (Psalm 119:32, NLT). "If you reject discipline, you only harm yourself; but if you listen to correction, you grow in understanding"* (Proverbs 15:32, NLT).

Bottom line: **I choose to trust you and your plan before understanding it.** (Because you are God and I am not.)

20

Gratitude

Thank you for your good plan . . .

You, the Creator of everything, are Sovereign, Providential, and Redemptive.
I am your loved child, redeemed by the blood of Jesus Christ and being transformed daily.
I choose to trust you and your plan before understanding it.
Thank you for your good plan and how you are working it out in my life.
Repenting of all known sin, I choose to live fully forgiven.
I forgive everyone for everything.
I cast every care on you.

How does a father bless his son? How does a son become a blessing to his father?

Consider Martin and his fourteen-year-old son, Jacob. As a successful business builder, Martin had all kinds of options for blessing his son; nothing was off the table. A generous allowance was the weekly habit, and although it was not specifically tied to a checklist of responsibilities, there was the expectation of diligence in schoolwork, respect for all family members, and a good attitude about helping with household chores. All was good.

Desiring to give Jake the best education possible, Martin enrolled him in the top private school in Denver at the beginning of his freshman year. It was a rocky start for Jake in a new environment with its already-established pecking order and secret alliances. But he adjusted, made friends, and gradually discovered that the world was a lot bigger than he had realized.

"What do you mean you can't play poker for 'that kind of money'?" his new buddy Andrew asked. "Doesn't your old man keep you supplied?"

"Of course he does," Jake insisted. "But I have better things to do with it."

"Baloney!" Andrew shot back. "I'll bet you don't even get $500 a week."

Jake flushed. At a loss for words, he turned and mumbled, "You don't know anything," and walked away.

Days turned into weeks, and Andrew's words ate at Jake. *How could I have been such a baby to think $50 a week was generous? Andrew is a screwup and he gets ten times more than me. It's not fair. I deserve better and here I am the one getting jerked over.*

Tension filled the air at home as Jake's bitterness grew, putting him at odds with everyone there, especially his dad. Finally, Martin said, "Jake, you and I need to talk."

It's about time, Jake thought. *I'll set things straight.* "Okay, talk," he said through a clenched jaw.

"Right there," Martin said. "That's an example. Your attitude lately has put everybody in pain. What's going on with you?"

"I'm sick of being treated like a baby. I think I'm a better son than any of my friends at school, but they get ten times my allowance. What did I do to deserve this?"

"I see," Martin said. "Anything else?"

"I just don't see how you expect me to be the model citizen and act happy all the time when you're not being fair with me."

"Well, maybe an adjustment is in order," Martin said.

"Good!" Jake answered. "I'm glad you see it that way."

"I think $25 a week should suffice," Martin said.

"Dad! A 25-dollar raise is hardly enough," Jake whined. "You have no idea . . . "

"I'm not talking about a $25 raise, Jake. I'm saying your allowance just went to $25 and I'm thinking about stopping it altogether. Fifty bucks a week might be better spent and more appreciated by Big Brothers Big Sisters. I've got some serious thinking to do."

How do you process this?

This story has many underlying principles and perspectives. We have a father who is concerned about the big picture and long-term character of his son. We have a son who feels entitled, at least temporarily. His ingratitude is embittering him against those who love him, poisoning the atmosphere in the home. And to make it more difficult, he feels justified in his position.

What do you see as the answer? I assume you're probably thinking as the father in this story, identifying with his role and trying to figure out an approach that will work. It's not easy being a parent. It's even tougher if you hope to keep your children happy all the time.

But I'd like you to shift gears for a moment. Put yourself in the kid's place. Not as a freshman in high school but as an imperfect child of God. What comparisons feed your discontentment? What unfairness are you saddled with? What role does ingratitude play in your inner dialogue?

Or, as I hope in your case, what habits are you deliberately developing to raise your awareness of reasons to be grateful?

A prize tool
Gratitude is a big deal. It may be your most powerful tool in the drive to enjoy life. More than just fending off bitterness, it may also be your most powerful weapon against anxiety and even the blahs. Although it is an emotion, it is neither random nor totally natural: it is the predictable result of proactive mental processing.

But not always. Sometimes it comes naturally, particularly with some new thrill. But as repetition removes the surprise and novelty, gratitude often fades. Expectation begins to push gratitude from centerstage to backstage. Then entitlement adds its growing muscle, and gratitude gets forced out of the house. Happiness, in the absence of gratitude, says, "I don't belong here anymore. All my air is gone. Hope we can meet again someday."

How do you stop the decay into expectation and entitlement? Proactive mental processing. But it's not about creating a mental image of all the good things you deserve so you can attract them from the universe. That's New Age philosophy in its various forms: deceptions that replace God with the power of self in a universe supposedly waiting to give you what you want.

In some ways, the truth is just the reverse. Recognizing that I am a speck in the universe, I am extremely grateful that God takes a beneficial interest in me. As David said in Psalm 8:3-4, *"When I look at the night sky and see the work of your fingers – the moon and the stars you set in place – what are mere mortals that you should think about them, human beings that you should care for them?"* (NLT).

Add to that the fact that whatever miniscule power I have is infected with sin. And God cares about me? How can I not be grateful? This is gratitude building on a foundation of humility that God can bless. *"God blesses those who are humble, for they will inherit the whole earth"* (Matthew 5:5, NLT).

Gratitude begets happiness

Here is a quick skeleton view of how gratitude gives rise to happiness.

1. I realize that I am marvelously created in the image of God.

2. I acknowledge that I fail miserably to love God with all my heart and my neighbor as myself. Instead, I am selfish, rebellious, self-justifying, and critical of others for the same defects I despise in myself. Understanding this is humility. It is also reality. Until I face it, I can never arrive at the right answer because the math just won't work.

3. God is totally aware of my weakness and loves me anyway. He recognizes that I am overmatched in my struggle against the evil lord of this world.

4. He promises me ultimate victory based not on my worthiness but the worthiness of his Son. He also assures me that he has a grand plan for my life – with its ups and downs – and that I can cooperate with him in working all things together for good.

5. I now (when I think right) choose to believe that even painful events are within God's grand plan – that in due time I will scratch my head and say, "I would never have believed how that pain would lead to something else and then to another something else and now, to this. What an amazing gift!"

6. If it takes longer than I want, and it usually does, I can be thankful for the opportunity to learn patience and contentment. (Did I really say that? This is a work in progress, you know. Don't expect perfection: Maria will verify that it's still a long way off.)

7. All of this enables me to have "Thank you" on my lips every time I pause to align my natural emotions with the reality of God's character and provision. This is gratitude based on trust giving birth to happiness. And it works.

Conscious practice

A few years ago I changed my life verse to this very short set of three verses because they openly declare that they are God's will for me. *"Rejoice always,* [17] *pray continually,* [18] *give thanks in all circum-*

stances; for this is God's will for you in Christ Jesus" (1 Thessalonians 5:16-18, NIV).

I have been focusing on these three simple commands: Rejoice, Pray, Give thanks. And it is revolutionizing the way I see life, the way I interpret its meaning, and the way I respond. As the old Bob Dylan song says, "It ain't me, babe." Not naturally, anyway, but it's what I'm becoming.

Now that I think about it, it's probably what paved the way for me to see the value in a credo that would go deeper yet in refining my worldview.

Closing thoughts

Expressing gratitude is the super vitamin of the soul, activating hope.

Gratitude is the logical follow-up to trust, putting circumstances back into perspective.

Frequent thank-yous lead to joy.

My happiness is dependent upon my gratitude and cannot exceed it.

21

God's Good Plan

Thank you for **your good plan** . . .

You, the Creator of everything, are Sovereign, Providential, and Redemptive.
I am your loved child, redeemed by the blood of Jesus Christ and being transformed daily.
I choose to trust you and your plan before understanding it.
Thank you for your good plan and how you are working it out in my life.
Repenting of all known sin, I choose to live fully forgiven.
I forgive everyone for everything.
I cast every care on you.

With my thanks I confirm my trust in the goodness of God's plan because of the goodness of God. His plan, when finally seen in its totality, will perfectly reflect his creative power, unfailing love, and patient character in working all things together for good.

How about your plans?

Your plans are meaningful.

Flowing through the filter of your worldview, your plans may be ambitious or cautious, carefully considered or relatively spontaneous. Reflecting your values, your intent, and your goals, they also demonstrate your foresight, your strategic thinking, your resourcefulness, your leadership, and your organizational skill. They say a lot about you because they reflect your heart.

Your plans are meaningless.

Okay, "meaningless" is an overstatement. But this is not: your plans always lack crucial information because you are neither omniscient nor omnipotent. On the battlefield, unexpected events within the first ten seconds can create a bottleneck that ruins your carefully arranged sequence of action. This is why Field Marshal Bernard von Moltke concluded, "No battle plan ever survives the first encounter with the enemy."

The moment your plan is launched, you are already in revision territory. You're having to adapt to one unintended consequence after another, to say nothing of the unanticipated responses of everyone else involved – including party crashers you could never have imagined on the scene. Where did they come from to invade your airtight plan?

If you were dealing only with stuff, the logistics might still be tricky, but it would be child's play compared to dealing with people.

In earlier chapters, we discussed the wild card of human free will – but only in relationship to a good creation gone rogue. Now consider how free will affects your ability to plan, because you're not operating in a vacuum. The free will of everyone on the planet is an endless chain of wild cards that you can neither predict nor disarm.

But still you plan. And you should, because as President Eisenhower said, "The plan is useless, but planning is essential." We understand this to mean that although the plan on paper may not survive "the first encounter with the enemy," all the preparation and forethought required to create the plan do several positive things that survive the plan itself. You are forced to refine your objective – what is the goal? You are forced to evaluate what you know about your enemy – their strengths and weaknesses.

Further, you are forced to think through a general strategy that remains viable even after tactical elements fail. You are forced to envision the resources you will need and how they will arrive when and where you need them. All of this prepares you mentally so that your on-the-fly adjustments are more like pre-reasoned responses than emotional knee-jerk reactions. So keep planning, but realize your limitations.

Here is how James describes it. *"Now listen, you who say, 'Today or tomorrow we will go to this or that city, spend a year there, carry on business and make money.' Why, you do not even know what will happen tomorrow. What is your life? You are a mist that appears for a little while and then vanishes. Instead, you ought to say, 'If it is the Lord's will, we will live and do this or that.' As it is, you boast in your arrogant schemes. All such boasting is evil"* (James 4:13-16, NIV).

The contrast between our plans and God's

I say all this to draw a contrast between our plans and God's plans. He is both omniscient and omnipotent. He lacks no crucial information. He sees the future as clearly as the present, because to him they are equally accessible. He perfectly anticipates the exercise of our free will, and he has countermoves that guarantee the success of his plan. He is the master chess player who invented the game. No matter what move his opponent makes, the master has a move that turns it to advantage.

God's plans for you

Let's start with one you knew was coming; you probably memorized it years ago. *"For I know the plans I have for you,' declares the Lord, 'plans to prosper you and not to harm you, plans to give you hope and a future'"* (Jeremiah 29:11, NIV).

And who would not want this long list of benefits God is waiting to grant those who seek and trust him? *"If you want better **insight and discernment**, and are searching for them as you would for **lost money or hidden treasure**, then **wisdom** will be given you and knowledge of God himself; you will soon learn the importance of reverence for the Lord and of **trusting him**. For the Lord grants wisdom! His every word is a **treasure of knowledge and understanding**. He grants **good sense** to the godly — his saints. He is their **shield, protecting them and guarding their pathway**. He shows how to **distinguish right from wrong**, how to **find the right decision every time**. For **wisdom and truth** will enter the very center of your being, filling your life with **joy**"* (Proverbs 2:3-10, TLB, emphasis added). I, for one, want a life filled with joy.

Now let's explore a similar list of benefits from the New Testament. These are Paul's requests on your behalf. I know you can read through the four lines in this passage from Colossians in a matter of seconds –

without anything really sinking in. But I urge you to consider the depth of meaning in words and phrases like "knit together with strong ties of love," "rich experience," "certainty and clear understanding," "God's secret plan," "hidden, mighty untapped treasures of wisdom and knowledge." This passage has way more value than chests of gold in a sunken pirate ship off the Caribbean coast of Cartagena. Read it slowly and let it sink in.

"This is what I have asked of God for you: that you will be encouraged and knit together by strong ties of love, and that you will have the rich experience of knowing Christ with real certainty and clear understanding. **For God's secret plan, now at last made known, is Christ himself.** *In him lie hidden all the mighty, untapped treasures of wisdom and knowledge"* (Colossians 2:2-3, TLB, emphasis added).

It makes perfect sense that in Christ would *"lie hidden all the mighty, untapped treasures of wisdom and knowledge"* – he created EVERYTHING!

And he wants you to have full and intimate access to himself. *"I am the vine; you are the branches. Those who remain in me, and I in them, will produce much fruit. For apart from me you can do nothing . . . I have loved you even as the Father has loved me. Remain in my love . . . I have told you these things so that you will be filled with my joy. Yes, your joy will overflow! This is my commandment: Love each other in the same way I have loved you"* (John 15:5-12, NLT).

How did he love us? In the greatest way possible. He took our sins upon himself, laid down his life, and took our place in judgment. All part of the Father's good plan for us, a plan for which Jesus volunteered *"for the joy that was set before him"* (Hebrews 12:2, NIV).

22

God Working out His Good Plan in My Life

Thank you for your good plan and how you are **working it out in my life.**

You, the Creator of everything, are Sovereign, Providential, and Redemptive.
I am your loved child, redeemed by the blood of Jesus Christ and being transformed daily.
I choose to trust you and your plan before understanding it.
Thank you for your good plan and how you are working it out in my life.
Repenting of all known sin, I choose to live fully forgiven.
I forgive everyone for everything.
I cast every care on you.

"For it is God who works in you to will and to act in order to fulfill his good purpose" (Philippians 2:13, NIV).

This is God's providence in action. He is the irresistible power behind both the plan and its execution. And he's doing it on the stage of your life – along with everyone else's. Amazingly complex and beyond human comprehension.

God's guidance

"The Lord says, 'I will guide you along the best pathway for your life. I will advise you and watch over you'" (Psalm 32:8, NLT).

Just look at that verse: what more could you ask for? But of course the value of the promise hinges on the capability of the one who makes it. Is it just a good intention without the horsepower to back it up? Is the promisor powerful? Is he trustworthy?

Let's frame the question this way: Is the creator of everything capable of guiding and protecting one of his chosen and loved children? The obvious answer is yes. But there is a bit of a hitch.

God never promises to force us into making only the best choices available to us. His promise is to guide, advise, and watch over. So the potential is always present for making only the best choices, but our free will is still operational.

We frequently manage to make inferior choices — perhaps not the worst but certainly not always the best. Sometimes we do it in ignorance because we haven't sufficiently sought the wisdom God has provided for us.

Other times, our inferior choices are deliberate. We may not recognize them as rebellious, but that is an appropriate label for going against our conscience to choose a selfish desire over one with a longer-term benefit. Like an addict, we sometimes choose a momentary pleasure that is not in our best interest.

When we ignore God's guidance

So what happens when we ignore God's guidance? Does he withdraw? Does he say, "I've had it with you. You're on your own"? Not exactly, although it can feel that way, because he *does* allow the pain of consequences to be one of our teachers. But he never abandons us.

This takes us back to his redemptive nature. When we confess and repent, he removes the eternal consequence of our guilt, but he doesn't rewrite history and remove the offensive incident from the movie of our life.

Instead, he redeems it. Like turning the tragedy of the crucifixion into the triumph of resurrection. None of the disciples, viewing the painful and humiliating death of their leader, could have imagined that 2,000-plus years later we would wear crosses as symbols of our victory in Christ over death.

Good, Better, Best

If you have put your trust in Christ alone to make you righteous – fully acceptable to Holy God – you can rest assured that he is working out his good plan in your life. Could it be better? Yes, to the degree you cooperate with him and make the best choices within the options available to you.

Think of it like your GPS guidance. When you miss a turn for whatever reason, it doesn't go offline and leave you to figure it out by yourself. It recalculates and gives you the best option from your current location. Sometimes it means a U-turn – but only if that's the best route from here to your destination.

Even more amazing, God is working out your route guidance along with everyone else's simultaneously – as he *"works all things together for good."*

Are you terminal?

Have you been diagnosed with a terminal condition? I don't mean the general one we all have, I mean a specific and unexpected one that has you on a short leash. How are you responding to it? How do you interpret its meaning? Its implications? Its significance? Are you filled with fear? Regret? Bitterness?

Or are you striving to fully trust in your loving Father to use even this in a way that will bring light to you and those you love? Are you looking for ultimate healing, whether it means prolonging your life on this earth or being released into the joy you were created to experience?

The quality of every day you have left will depend on how you interpret God's good plan for you and the depth of your trust in how he is working it out in your life.

This powerful poem by Corrie ten Boom helped change my perspective years ago.

My life is but a weaving between my God and me.
I cannot choose the colors, He weaveth steadily.
Oft' times He weaveth sorrow; and I in foolish pride
Forget He sees the upper and I, the underside.

Not 'til the loom is silent and the shuttles cease to fly
Will God unroll the canvas and reveal the reason why
The dark threads are as needful in the weaver's skillful hand
As the threads of gold and silver in the pattern He has planned.

He knows, He loves, He cares; nothing this truth can dim.
He gives the very best to those who leave the choice to Him.

Don't let the power of the last line escape you. Only God is capable of making the best choice. How could it be otherwise? Keeping him out of the loop is like facing a momentous decision and accepting a coin toss rather than guidance from the expert – who just happens to know the future and everything else as well. He wants the best for you. If you force your own will over his, you always settle for less than the best.

Revisiting why God doesn't do more

In further answer to the question of why God doesn't do more to eliminate suffering, consider how he is working out his plan in your life. He has paid you the honor of making you (along with all believers) his body. He has commissioned us to be his hands and feet, his ambassadors.

When we ask, "Why aren't you doing more?" he asks, "Why aren't YOU doing more? I have given you every provision to care for each other and meet each other's needs. I am treating you as full partners. In fact, I allow my reputation on earth to be determined by your actions. The world judges me by what it sees you doing – and not doing.

"Would you prefer that I demote you to the level of animal or plant life that carries no such responsibility or honor? Begin doing what Jesus did. Step out in faith for the sake of your neighbors and the honor of my name. I will bless your efforts with success. And in the process, you will discover the greatest fulfillment possible in this life – to say nothing of storing up treasure for all eternity. This is how I am working out my plan in your life along with everyone else's."

23

When the Plan Doesn't Seem So Good

Thank you for your good plan and how you are **working it out in my life.**

You, the Creator of everything, are Sovereign, Providential, and Redemptive.
I am your loved child, redeemed by the blood of Jesus Christ and being transformed daily.
I choose to trust you and your plan before understanding it.
Thank you for your good plan and how you are working it out in my life.
Repenting of all known sin, I choose to live fully forgiven.
I forgive everyone for everything.
I cast every care on you.

"For we are God's handiwork, created in Christ Jesus to do good works, which God prepared in advance for us to do" (Ephesians 2:10, NIV).

What if the plan isn't working for you?

I get it. And I will resist asking the question, "Whose fault is that?" because I think you, like most people, are doing the best you know how to do most of the time.

Your daily actions continuously build on previously established patterns as they create new ones. Knowing that these harden over time, prudent people strive to build patterns that will help them gain perspective, interpret events, and improve their life.

Others simply react to events based only on what seems good in the moment. Still others feel stuck with a script they have been handed – not recognizing it for what it is: a setting with a fixed backstory and developing characters. They are not obligated to play any stereotype character, and even their suggested lines are not written in stone. Each new dawn can begin a new scene, a new chapter, a new act, a new direction.

But still, there are moments when it feels like you're being unfairly punished. Here is some advice from the prophet Jeremiah. *"When life is heavy and hard to take, go off by yourself. Enter the silence. Bow in prayer. Don't ask questions: Wait for hope to appear. Don't run from trouble. Take it full-face. The 'worst' is never the worst"* (Lamentations 3:28-30, MSG).

"For no one is abandoned by the Lord forever. Though he brings grief, he also shows compassion because of the greatness of his unfailing love. For he does not enjoy hurting people or causing them sorrow" (Lamentations 3:31-33, NLT).

Trying to see the reasons behind it

The reasons that will be revealed in due time will be more than satisfactory, but until then they remain a mystery, unable to relieve your suffering in the present. And even if someone could tell you right now exactly what those reasons are, you would be unlikely to appreciate their true value: they would feel thin and flimsy compared to your present pain.

This is due in part to the natural tendency to overestimate pain in the present and underestimate its reality in the future. Scientific studies show that most people will gladly agree to accept a greater future pain in trade for relief from a lesser pain today.

It's the same principle that drives most people to accept a lesser benefit if they can get it today rather than a greater benefit that must be delayed. This is because the future seems less real to us than the present – even though the future, when we finally experience it, will be every bit as real as our present experience.

This perceptual distortion is probably related to the fact that our experience of life is in the ever-unfolding now. Nothing past or future seems as real as this moment because it is only in this moment that we have the power to act.

It's all relative

One benefit of this is that although an hour's acute pain can seem like a lifetime of agony, it is soon forgotten. The reason I raise this point is to demonstrate one of the difficulties of measuring whether the plan you're in right now is beneficial – even if it doesn't feel like it in the moment.

This is how Paul explained it to the believers in Corinth. *"That is why we never give up. Though our bodies are dying, our spirits are being renewed every day. For our present troubles are small and won't last very long. Yet they produce for us a glory that vastly outweighs them and will last forever! So we don't look at the troubles we can see now; rather, we fix our gaze on things that cannot be seen. For the things we see now will soon be gone, but the things we cannot see will last forever"* (2 Corinthians 4:16-18, NLT).

Fix your gaze on the big picture

What if you are in a time of discipline or correction? Painful for the moment but extremely valuable in the big picture, it's one of many seasons you can look back on and say, "I never want to be there again, but I am so grateful God took me through it."

Or what if you are in a time of training for a major challenge that you know nothing about at this point – a challenge that will result in a great victory if you are properly prepared for it? Think Olympics: a lot of disciplined effort and pain precede that performance on a worldwide stage.

This reality led Paul to encourage the believers in Rome with these words: *"We can rejoice, too, when we run into problems and trials, for we know that they help us develop endurance. And endurance develops strength of character, and character strengthens our confident hope of salvation"* (Romans 5:3-4, NLT).

Jesus not only understood the principle but also acted on it. In spite of the fears he encountered in the Garden of Gethsemane, he kept his eye on the big picture and continued to entrust his life and welfare to the Father's plan. *"Because of the joy awaiting him, he endured the cross, disregarding its shame. Now he is seated in the place of honor beside God's throne"* (Hebrews 12:2, NLT).

Tough questions

Do you have the wisdom to trade a lesser pleasure now for a greater one in the future? Have you experienced the pleasure that comes from training your tastes to appreciate what is good for you and to dislike – or at least discount – the things that are bad for you? Yes, I'm talking about food at the moment, but the principle applies to everything else as well.

How do you measure (in the big picture) the meaning or value of a day, week, month, year, decade, or even your lifetime? How do you value the example you provide for your children, grandchildren and beyond? What would your lineage look like if you had not played your role?

What if your role is to demonstrate trust and joy in the context of extraordinary suffering? Can God supernaturally provide what you need if he calls you to that level of service? Can he reward your trust with extraordinary joy? I'm counting on it.

I often think back to the inspiring words of Habakkuk: *"Even though the fig trees have no blossoms, and there are no grapes on the vines; even though the olive crop fails, and the fields lie empty and barren; even though the flocks die in the fields, and the cattle barns are empty, yet **I will rejoice in the Lord! I will be joyful in the God of my salvation! The Sovereign Lord is my strength!*** *He makes me as surefooted as a deer, able to tread upon the heights"* (Habakkuk 3:17-19, NLT, emphasis added).

How do you think God measures the value of human time with regard to what he is doing in your big picture, which vastly exceeds human time? He certainly doesn't look at your hours and weeks and years as meaningless, but he is certainly aware of how they pale in significance to what they will accrue for you in eternity.

Accordingly, he is willing to make beneficial trades in your pain account that will not seem to you to be beneficial at all – at least not in the present.

How might your experience – even suffering – provide a pivotal point in the life of your family and beyond? Can you trust God with what you cannot yet see – how he is working out his plan in your life? *"Now we see things imperfectly, like puzzling reflections in a mirror, but then we will see everything with perfect clarity. All that I know now is partial and incomplete, but then I will know everything completely, just as God now knows me completely"* (1 Corinthians 13:12, (NLT).

How Paul dealt with a plan that didn't seem to be working for him

After his conversion from persecuting and even executing Christians, Paul entered an extended time of serious training. He emerged as a motivated communicator of the gospel, writing much of the New Testament.

In addition to enduring beatings, imprisonment, and all kinds of hardships, he was weakened by a physical condition of some kind.

Three times he prayed for God's healing. Three times he got God's answer: *"No. But I am with you; that is all you need. My power shows up best in weak people."*

Here is Paul's amazing response: *"Now I am glad to boast about how weak I am; I am glad to be a living demonstration of Christ's power, instead of showing off my own power and abilities"* (2 Corinthians 12:9, TLB).

Paul understood that this present moment – even our entire life – is chickenfeed compared to the big picture. See what he says in his letter to the Romans, *"I consider that our present sufferings are not worth comparing with the glory that will be revealed in us. For the creation waits in eager expectation for the children of God to be revealed"* (Romans 8:18-19, NIV).

Peter encourages us with these words. *"So be truly glad. There is wonderful joy ahead, even though you must endure many trials for a little while. These trials will show that your faith is genuine. It is being tested as fire tests and purifies gold – though your faith is far more precious than mere gold. So when your faith remains strong through many trials, it will bring you much praise and glory and honor on the day when Jesus Christ is revealed to the whole world"* (1 Peter 1:6-7, NLT).

24

The Positive Response of Repentance

Repenting of all known sin . . .

You, the Creator of everything, are Sovereign, Providential, and Redemptive.
I am your loved child, redeemed by the blood of Jesus Christ and being transformed daily.
I choose to trust you and your plan before understanding it.
Thank you for your good plan and how you are working it out in my life.
Repenting of all known sin, I choose to live fully forgiven.
I forgive everyone for everything.
I cast every care on you.

"Repent therefore, and turn back, that your sins may be blotted out" (Acts 3:19, ESV).

The meaning of repentance

It's interesting how dictionaries define the word "repent." Most modern dictionaries define it as feeling sorry or regretful about past actions. Webster, a dictionary with a Christian history, comes much closer to a biblical perspective. It offers three definitions:

> 1: "to turn from sin and dedicate oneself to the amendment of one's life"
>
> 2a: "to feel regret or contrition"
>
> 2b: "to change one's mind"

The first one is most like the Old Testament view. The second is the current popular view and reflects most dictionaries. The third is most like the New Testament view.

Notice that the command to repent in Acts 3:19 adds the specific clause, *"and turn back."* This is like saying, "Just in case your idea of repentance is merely feeling sorry – or even the stronger idea of changing your mind about right and wrong – I want to make it clear that I am calling you to action. Make a U-turn. You can't undo what you've done, but you can disengage and distance yourself from any further relationship to that activity and its perceived benefits. Make it decisive. Do a 180 now."

"Or do you presume on the riches of his kindness and forbearance and patience, not knowing that God's kindness is meant to lead you to repentance?" (Romans 2:4, ESV).

God's heart regarding repentance

First things first. Everything God does with regard to humans is for their benefit – his commands, his restrictions, his discipline – everything. When we don't see it that way in any given instance, it is because our vision is limited by ignorance and darkened by Satan's deceptions.

Even imperfect human parents love their children and want them to experience a meaningful, fulfilling life. They grieve when they see their children make bad choices that will end up hurting them and limiting their future. They rejoice when their children realize it and make a new start. How do you think God chooses to deal with you, his loved child? Here is one clue: *"Those whom I love, I reprove and discipline, so be zealous and repent"* (Revelation 3:19, ESV). This sounds like he loves you enough to use pain, if necessary, to protect your future welfare by moving you toward repentance.

Repentance as a gift from God

Isn't it fascinating that although man repents, God is the one granting the ability? *". . . God may perhaps grant them repentance leading to a knowledge of the truth, and they may come to their senses and escape from the snare of the devil, after being captured by him to do his will"* (2 Timothy 2:25-26, ESV).

We have another example of God inspiring human repentance in the Acts Chapter 11 story of the first Gentile converts. Peter reports to his legalistic Jewish peers that God gave him a vision and led him to the home of a Gentile to share the gospel.

The Spirit of God fell on the household, confirming that God was behind this. Peter reported, *"If then God gave the same gift to them as he gave to us when we believed in the Lord Jesus Christ, who was I that I could stand in God's way?"*

The response of the legalists is remarkable: *"When they heard these things they fell silent. And they glorified God, saying, 'Then to the Gentiles also God has granted* **repentance that leads to life***'"* (Acts 11:18, ESV, emphasis added).

Here is the point: even the ability to repent is a gift from God. And it leads to life. But unless God grants it, the Gentiles (all humans for that matter) would not be able to repent. Either it would not occur to them or they would find it too distasteful. Repentance is like medicine, meant to heal, not to taste like candy. And God's desire is to heal you.

Why God desires repentance
Do you think God prefers to condemn or to forgive? Does he favor justice or mercy? Does he want you to get what's coming to you or does he want to pardon you?

Even the Old Testament points to God's compassionate desire to give life and blessing. Listen as he pleads with Israel through Moses: *"Today I have given you the choice between life and death, between blessings and curses. Now I call on heaven and earth to witness the choice you make. Oh, that you would choose life, so that you and your descendants might live! You can make this choice by loving the Lord your God, obeying him, and committing yourself firmly to him. This is the key to your life. And if you love and obey the Lord, you will live long in the land . . ."* (Deuteronomy 30:19-20, NLT).

Jesus emphasizes the same theme in his conversation with Nicodemus. Speaking of himself, he says, *"For God did not send his Son into the world to condemn the world, but in order that the world might be saved through him"* (John 3:17, ESV).

Later, he reveals more of his desire: *"I came that they may have life and have it abundantly"* (John 10:10, ESV).

Repentance as the gateway into God's blessing
Since he regards us this way, and repentance is the gateway into his blessing, why do we avoid it? It seems rather obvious that our pride resists admitting

that we are flawed and guilty, that we are not self-sufficient in our own righteousness. Meanwhile, Jesus gives us this glimpse of heaven pulling for us: *"I tell you, there is joy before the angels of God over one sinner who repents"* (Luke 15:10, ESV).

Man's pattern regarding repentance

"And yet the people of Israel keep saying, 'The Lord isn't doing what's right!' O people of Israel, it is you who are not doing what's right, not I. Therefore, I will judge each of you, O people of Israel, according to your actions, says the Sovereign Lord. Repent, and turn from your sins. Don't let them destroy you! Put all your rebellion behind you, and find yourselves a new heart and a new spirit. For why should you die, O people of Israel?" (Ezekiel 18:29-31, ESV).

God pleads with his people for their own benefit and yet they resist. What an amazing picture this is: the Creator wants to bless but is restrained by the creature's own choice.

Fallen free will strikes again. And the pattern continues. *"But in spite of this, the people kept sinning. Despite his wonders, they refused to trust him. So he ended their lives in failure, their years in terror. When God began killing them, they finally sought him. They repented and took God seriously. Then they remembered that God was their rock, that God Most High was their redeemer"* (Psalm 78:32-35, NLT).

Finally! They come to their senses. Oops. *"But all they gave him was lip service; they lied to him with their tongues. Their hearts were not loyal to him. They did not keep his covenant."* (Psalm 78:36-37, NLT).

Here we go again. *"Yet he was merciful and forgave their sins and did not destroy them all. Many times he held back his anger and did not unleash his fury! For he remembered that they were merely mortal, gone like a breath of wind that never returns"* (Psalm 78:38-39, NLT).

What patience! Here is how Peter states it: *". . . He [God] is being patient for your sake. He does not want anyone to be destroyed, but wants everyone to repent"* (2 Peter 3:9, NLT).

Do we trust God to keep his promises?
If we trust the word of the Creator of everything, why would we not repent when he assures us of this outcome? *"If we confess our sins, he is faithful and just to forgive us our sins and to cleanse us from all unrighteousness"* (1 John 1:9, ESV).

Repenting of all known sin
Jesus said, ". . . unless you repent, you will all likewise perish" (Luke 13:5, ESV). Of what am I to repent? At the risk of oversimplifying, let me suggest three categories of sin in my life: (1) the sin I am aware of because my own conscience condemns me; (2) the sin I excuse by rationalizing that it's just human nature, or everyone does it, or I can't help myself, or it could be worse, etc.; (3) the sin I am not even aware of that misses the mark of God's perfect standard.

The Peace Credo's intentional wording of "all known sin" focuses on the first two categories of sin. This is not because the third category is meaningless but because the first two will keep most of us busy most of the time. As we make serious progress with those, God will enable us to see other areas where repentance will lead us to greater freedom from bondage and more joyful fellowship with him.

David's response to God's call to repentance must have been part of the reason he was called a man after God's own heart. Look at his proactive request for God to reveal even the third category of sin in his life: *"Search me, O God, and know my heart; test me and know my anxious thoughts. Point out anything in me that offends you, and lead me along the path of everlasting life"* (Psalm 139:23-24, NLT).

Finally, imagine the feeling of relief, freedom, and joy David felt when God kept his promise to forgive and cleanse. *"Finally, I confessed all my sins to you and stopped trying to hide my guilt. I said to myself, 'I will confess my rebellion to the Lord.' And you forgave me! All my guilt is gone"* (Psalm 32:5, NLT).

When our response mirrors David's, we can rejoice in the same freedom: *"You forgave me! All my guilt is gone!"*

25

The Boogeyman

Repenting of all known sin, **I choose to live fully forgiven.**

You, the Creator of everything, are Sovereign, Providential, and Redemptive.
I am your loved child, redeemed by the blood of Jesus Christ and being transformed daily.
I choose to trust you and your plan before understanding it.
Thank you for your good plan and how you are working it out in my life.
Repenting of all known sin, I choose to live fully forgiven.
I forgive everyone for everything.
I cast every care on you.

"Even if we feel guilty, God is greater than our feelings, and he knows everything" (1 John 3:20, NLT).

The guilt God can't forgive

As a student at Wheaton College, I took a few Bible courses. I'll never forget one exam that occurred during a particularly busy time when I couldn't prepare sufficiently. (Interpretation: I screwed up. My misplaced priorities kept me from reading all the required material.)

One of the questions was, "What can God not forgive?" I was excited to finally see a question I could answer with confidence. A single word was all I needed. "Nothing!"

When the graded tests were returned, I scanned through the disappointing results and was shocked to find that I had totally missed the one question I was so sure of. My prof, Dr. Gordon Fee, had scratched a brief note next to my answer. *"God cannot forgive irrational guilt, because it isn't real."*

It was an eye opener for me, and I am grateful to this day.

Irrational guilt
There is a lot of unnecessary pain in the world because of irrational guilt. This is a feeling that is not from God. It may be the result of Satan's bogus accusations. It could be from a misunderstanding, maybe a wrong teaching you picked up somewhere. Or maybe you have an overactive conscience because of a stronghold of fear.

Most important, it could be that you don't believe God has kept his promise to forgive you. Perhaps knowing you don't deserve his forgiveness looms too large in your mind, overpowering his grace that delights in giving you better than you deserve.

Regardless of the combination of these that could be plaguing you, the verse at the top of this chapter applies: *"Even if we feel guilty, God is greater than our feelings, and he knows everything."* I can't emphasize this strongly enough: Don't allow your feelings to invalidate God's truth!

However, I never want to dismiss a feeling of guilt too quickly by simply labeling it irrational. I am convinced that most feelings of guilt for most people are legitimate signals that we have violated God's standard in some way. The feelings are warnings to do something about it before we do further damage to ourselves or others.

Guilt, feelings of guilt, and the boogeyman of shame

- Guilt is a simple fact: you're guilty of doing something wrong. Guilt says, "I did wrong."
- Feelings of guilt naturally accompany the fact of guilt in a healthy person. The feeling says, "I feel bad about the wrong I did."
- Shame takes the feeling of guilt and turns it into a general self-condemnation. Shame says, "I am wrong. I am bad." And in the words of author Brene Brown, "I am unworthy of love, belonging, and connection." Keep in mind, of course, that until we are born again, the shame totally fits: we are wrong, bad, lost, and without hope.

Guilt

This chapter's focus is not about your guilt: it's about living forgiven. It assumes that you have dealt with your guilt through repentance, the topic of the last chapter.

Please don't take this chapter to imply that guilt is imaginary or irrelevant. We all have personal guilt. We all stand justly condemned because of it. God alone has the power to remove our guilt. Fortunately, he also has the desire. This chapter assumes that you are keeping short accounts with God and repenting of sin as you become aware of it.

How many times have you seen the dreaded "Check engine" light on the dashboard of your car? How many times did it coincide with an immediate shutdown? Probably never. So you could ignore it, right?

Eventually, one of two things happens, neither one of which is okay. One possibility is that when you finally get around to having it checked, the damage may have gone from under a hundred dollars to repair to hundreds or even thousands. If you wait long enough, the other possibility kicks in: the engine actually shuts down, ruining your schedule and leaving you stranded.

Keeping short accounts with God is like routine maintenance: not unimportant or optional. Don't let guilt pile up and start oozing slime.

Feelings of guilt

If you are relatively normal, most of your feelings of guilt have good cause for existence. God is communicating that you need maintenance. Something is polluting your system, interrupting your relationship with him, and destroying your peace.

Although the feeling is painful, it is a gift from God, much like the nerve endings in your body. They are designed to protect you by sensing danger and sending your brain a signal that it interprets as pain, prompting you to withdraw from the threat (Get your hand off the hot burner!).

We can't honestly eliminate our painful feelings of guilt without eliminating the guilt itself. Denial doesn't work, because at a deep level we know the truth, regardless of how we try to cover it up. Same with excusing. So how do we eliminate guilt? By confessing to God and repenting, and then by making restitution with those we have offended.

People may or may not forgive us, but God always forgives when we honestly repent. And God is the only one who, when he forgives us, also cleanses us *"from all unrighteousness"* (1 John 1:9, ESV).

The boogeyman of shame
Here is where it gets especially tricky. Earlier I said that irrational guilt may be the result of Satan's bogus accusations. That's true, but there is more to the story. Not all of Satan's accusations are bogus. If they were, you would feel righteously indignant at his lies and slander. But you wouldn't feel shame, because you would know the charges are false. You are not guilty.

Unfortunately, Satan doesn't have to manufacture bogus charges against you: he has plenty of legitimate charges, instances where you have given in to his temptations and violated God's character and your own conscience. His goal is to trigger shame in you that says, "I can never be good enough. God can never accept me. I am worthless. I am hopeless."

Hopelessness is not the end game: it gets worse
If you stay there, he wins. But then he doubles down, hoping for an even bigger win. He jumps on your feelings of hopelessness and tries to nudge you toward bitterness and open rebellion. This dangerous condition says, "God is unreasonable, impossible. I don't even believe he exists. I hate him."

This is part of a natural progression that Paul describes in the opening chapter of Romans. *"Since they thought it foolish to acknowledge God, he abandoned them to their foolish thinking . . . Their lives became full of every kind of wickedness . . . haters of God"* (Romans 1:28-30, NLT).

Good News!
"And such were some of you. But you were washed, you were sanctified, you were justified in the name of the Lord Jesus Christ and by the Spirit of our God" (1 Corinthians 16:11, ESV). This is why the gospel is such good news. It offers the only lasting solution to our problem of guilt and shame.

The entry into the solution is bloody: literally for Jesus, figuratively for us. We are forced to acknowledge our guilt and our complete inability to stop violating even our own conscience, let alone the unyielding standard of an omniscient, holy God.

If we could just turn over a new leaf and never sin again, we could understand God giving us a pass on the past. But we can't. At least I can't. Greater willpower doesn't cut it. The only option with any hope is a word that slices deeply into my pride: the word is "surrender." I admit my selfish actions and the fact that I can't fix them – either in the past or present.

The good news of the gospel is that God is waiting with open arms for me to exercise my free will and walk through his singular entrance to lasting inner peace.

He knows the burden I'm trying to carry, and he knows I am inadequate. That's why Jesus says, *"Come to me, all of you who are weary and carry heavy burdens, and I will give you rest"* (Matthew 11:28, NLT).

26

Living Fully Forgiven – Passport to Freedom

Repenting of all known sin, I choose to **live fully forgiven.**

> You, the Creator of everything, are Sovereign, Providential, and Redemptive.
> I am your loved child, redeemed by the blood of Jesus Christ and being transformed daily.
> I choose to trust you and your plan before understanding it.
> Thank you for your good plan and how you are working it out in my life.
> **Repenting of all known sin, I choose to live fully forgiven.**
> I forgive everyone for everything.
> I cast every care on you.

The charges against you: from bogus to real and back again

In the last chapter, we discussed Satan's bogus accusations. As problematic as they can be, they pale in comparison to the ones that really stick: the ones that align with the facts of our guilt. Their ongoing power to defeat us warrants giving them a closer look.

The accuser's last stand

Shame is the culprit here, and you are especially susceptible to it when you know the accusations against you have merit, that they are not totally bogus. But this is what you have to remember: Satan's shame-producing accusations – even the legitimate ones – are bogus in one important sense. They are obsolete. They are ghosts of the past he conjures up to haunt you and derail your growth.

Think about it: your guilt no longer exists if it has been forgiven by God. Not only your actions but even your old nature has been nailed to the cross. *"You were dead because of your sins and because your sinful nature was not yet cut away. Then God made you alive with Christ, for he forgave all our sins. He canceled the record of the charges against us and took it away by nailing it to the cross"* (Colossians 2:13-14, NLT). Your debt has been canceled. You are free.

"God made him who had no sin to be sin for us, so that in him we might become the righteousness of God" (2 Corinthians 5:21, NIV). So what happens when Satan points his finger at you? You may cower in the corner in fear of being exposed, but God answers, "What are you pointing at, Satan? There's no sin there. My Son took it. It's gone. It exists only in your sick memory. Leave my righteous child alone."

Confusion in the transformation process

In Chapter 15 we differentiated between how our condition and character change in the transformation process. Our condition changes immediately from condemned to pardoned, from sinful to righteous in God's sight. *"For he has clothed me with garments of salvation and arrayed me in a robe of his righteousness"* (Isaiah 61:10, NIV).

But our character changes slowly, day by day, as our old nature reluctantly gives way to the new. Here's how Paul describes it: *"I have discovered this principle of life – that when I want to do what is right,*

I inevitably do what is wrong. I love God's law with all my heart. But there is another power within me that is at war with my mind. This power makes me a slave to the sin that is still within me" (Romans 7:21-23, NLT).

This causes confusion for us since we are unable to see the righteous version of ourselves. We see only the mixed character side of the equation – and it is painfully inconsistent.

We are daily confronted with our internal war. Part of us wants to put God first in our life, and part of us wants our own selfish way. Over and over we see ourselves failing to do what we know is right. Conclusion? We feel like pathetic failures with no hope of consistently pleasing God.

But wait. God sees what you can't. He sees you differently. It's not that he is unaware of your failures, but he sees what he is helping you become.

He also sees the version of you that will inhabit eternity. He sees you covered in the righteousness of his Son, the Passover Lamb who took your place in judgment. *"Yet now he has reconciled you to himself through the death of Christ in his physical body. As a result, he has brought you into his own presence, and you are holy and blameless as you stand before him without a single fault"* (Colossians 1:22, NLT).

If God declares you *"holy and blameless,"* don't argue with his ability to forgive and cleanse. You haven't shown up holy and blameless in this timebound world yet, but God sees way beyond that. Trust his vision over your own.

The power of feelings

Your feelings will frequently attempt to invalidate God's truth, and they will do it from all directions. Before you sin, they whine: "What you want to do isn't so bad; it's normal. God can't be serious about saying no." After you sin, they nag you: "You rotten sinner. You need to pay for this. Why should you think God will forgive you?"

Feelings rule the day more often than we realize. As with so many other issues, we can see feelings ruling others but remain blind to it in ourselves. Our slightest attempt to think through an issue convinces us that we are doing it justice, coming to a logical conclusion rather than a selfish rationalization.

But often our logical analysis is no more than window dressing for an emotional preference. And emotional preferences are usually stacked in favor of the moment rather than the long term.

How aware are you of the pull of your emotions influencing your decisions? Awareness is the first step in cooperating with God to bring positive change.

Forgiving yourself

We hear a lot these days about forgiving yourself. Some of it is good, some of it not so good. Clearly, you have no power to forgive yourself OF sin, in the sense of removing it. Only God can do that.

But you can't fully accept and live in his forgiveness if you remain in the prison of your own shame that continues to shackle what God has set free. *"If the Son sets you free, you will be free indeed"* (John 8:36, ESV).

Declare your blood-bought freedom and reject Satan's obsolete accusations – no matter how factually accurate they once were. *"So now there is no condemnation for those who belong to Christ Jesus. And because you belong to him, the power of the life-giving Spirit **has freed you** from the power of sin that leads to death"* (Romans 8:1-2, NLT, emphasis added).

Choosing to live fully forgiven

Despite the daily struggle for your mixed character to live up to your identity as a child of God, your sin has been eliminated from God's sight. It is gone. He has removed the sin from your account, and his judgment is final: Not guilty! *"Therefore, if anyone is in Christ, the new creation has come: The old has gone, the new is here!"* (2 Corinthians 5:17, NIV).

It's time to reject the shame from guilt God has already forgiven. You are no longer a slave to sin and shame. You are a loved and redeemed child of God, being transformed daily. Live in freedom. Choose to live fully forgiven.

"Now to him who is able to keep you from stumbling and to present you blameless before the presence of his glory with great joy, to the only God, our Savior, through Jesus Christ our Lord, be glory, majesty, dominion, and authority, before all time and now and forever. Amen." (Jude 24-25, ESV).

27

Getting People off Your Hook

I forgive everyone for everything.

You, the Creator of everything, are Sovereign, Providential, and Redemptive.
I am your loved child, redeemed by the blood of Jesus Christ and being transformed daily.
I choose to trust you and your plan before understanding it.
Thank you for your good plan and how you are working it out in my life.
Repenting of all known sin, I choose to live fully forgiven.
I forgive everyone for everything.
I cast every care on you.

Have you noticed that we are incapable of living in relationship with other people without conflict? We compete with each other on many levels, and despite our best efforts we often experience a conflict of interests.

Conflicts of interest would never pose a problem if both parties were willing to give up their "rights" and defer to the other. Why don't we automatically deal with all conflicts this way?

We are quick to claim our concern for fairness. Maybe even moral purity or righteousness. But most of the time the primary concern is usually our own welfare and desires. We just don't like admitting it.

We are all selfish creatures. It comes naturally in our fallen state. One mark of maturity is awareness and respect for the needs of others. We all have that in varying degrees. But because none of us is perfect, conflict is inevitable. God has given us a means for dealing with it. He has taught it, commanded it, and demonstrated it Himself. It is one of the greatest keys to any fulfilling relationship.

Jesus taught: *"And when you stand praying, if you hold anything against anyone, forgive them, so that your Father in heaven may forgive you your sins"* (Mark 11:25, NIV).

Then in Romans 12:19, Paul adds, *"Never take revenge. Leave that to the righteous anger of God. For the Scriptures say, 'I will take revenge; I will pay them back,' says the Lord"* (NLT).

Let's attempt some immediate application by beginning with a somewhat unpleasant but necessary inventory. Please give this exercise at least a few minutes of serious thought. This could lead to inner peace for some long-buried hurts. It could also release you from chains of bondage to people you've buried alive.

When you harbor resentment — no matter how justified — your spirit, soul, and body all pay a price. It doesn't matter whether the people are from your distant past or the outer fringes of your life. Take time to answer these questions with real names, even if they have passed on.

- Who owes you an apology?
- Who hasn't repaid their debt to you?
- Who has said untrue things about you?
- Who insulted you in a way that really hurt?
- Who holds power over you?
- Who has hurt your career ambitions?
- Who has cheated you financially?
- Who has cheated you in games, sports, or a hobby?

- Who stole the person you thought would be the love of your life?
- Who has been unfaithful to you?
- Who has sued you?
- Who has hurt your children?
- Who has injured you due to negligence?
- Who has refused to help when you really needed it?
- Who has stolen from you?
- Who has broken an important promise to you?
- Who has treated you unfairly?

As names come to mind, do you get an uneasy feeling with any of them? Are there any with whom you feel a desire to get even? Perhaps you merely wish that they would somehow get a taste of justice or at least a hint of what you've suffered at their hands.

Are there any that you would avoid – even at a cost – rather than see them again? Are there any you have spoken negatively about? Have you influenced friends or family to join you in your offense against them?

A yes to any of these questions is a likely indicator that you have some folks on your hook. Welcome to humanity.

FAQs

Q1: Why should I forgive people who have clearly wronged me? I'm not talking about accidents; I'm talking about things I'm sure they did on purpose. They don't deserve my forgiveness.

A1: The "Why" should be clear later in this chapter and the next. The specific objection you're raising is that they don't deserve your forgiveness. You're right.

They don't. But that has nothing to do with it, because true forgiveness is NEVER deserved. Behavior can be excused, and debts can be repaid, but serious offenses cannot be undone; they can only be forgiven. Do you want to invite God to forgive you only when you deserve it? You would still be dead in your sins with no hope for appeal.

Q2: Won't forgiving them be like justifying what they did? That will just make them think they can do it again.

A2: No, forgiving them does not justify anything. The act of letting them off *your* hook lands them squarely on God's hook. And he is the only one capable of dealing adequately with them — for two reasons. First, he perfectly knows every detail, including their knowledge and motivation (culpability in legal terms). Second, he is omnipotent, unlimited in his power to deliver justice.

Remember that when God forgives sinners, he does it without ever justifying their sinful acts. He hates the sin while loving the sinner (fortunately for us!).

God then justifies sinners who repent and ask Jesus to pardon them. But he doesn't ask us to justify them; only he has the power to do that. Forgiving never implies that what they did was okay. If it was okay, it wouldn't need to be forgiven.

As far as repeat offenses, we have no guarantee, but God may use our forgiveness as an example of light in the process of transforming the offender.

Q3: How can I forgive them when I know I will never again be able to trust them?

A3: Forgiving doesn't require trust. Trust is a totally separate matter. You may forgive fully and trust only partially or not at all. There are good reasons to forgive even when there is no reason to trust.

Q4: Why can't I just let God do the forgiving if he wants to? Why should I have to do it?

A4: Because God commands you to forgive as well. And he does it for your own good. Your unwillingness to forgive does not preserve justice; it only poisons your own soul and keeps you in bondage. The power to forgive is essential to your spiritual, mental, and physical health. Failure to use it regularly is an underlying cause of many psychosomatic illnesses.

Forgiveness in three phases

Phase 1 is deciding whether to forgive. Phase 2 is granting forgiveness. Phase 3 is the aftermath, everything that follows.

Phase 1

This is a high hurdle. Deciding whether to forgive can be an agonizing choice, and the wrong conclusion will keep you from the victory that waits on the other side. Unfortunately, you can easily end up deciding whether to forgive based on whether you feel like it. Satan will try to confuse the matter by suggesting that it would be hypocrisy to forgive when forgiving is the last thing you feel like doing. "Who are you trying to kid?" he says. "You don't really mean it; it will never work."

Emotions are clearly suspect in this decision process. They enter it with a strong bias and must be dealt with accordingly. Since you have been hurt, your emotions typically respond with two goals in mind: self-preservation and revenge. Be on guard for the kinds of statements your emotions will throw at you:

- You'll regret this. If you forgive them, they'll just do it to you again.
- Why should you have to do the hard work of forgiving? You're the one who was wronged.
- Don't let them off the hook.
- They deserve to hurt. Don't make it too easy.
- Let's just ignore them. We can even the score without actually doing anything.

Since our feelings can easily dissuade us from deciding to forgive, the decision should be based on something more objective and reliable. How is this for direction? Jesus said, *"For if you forgive other people when they sin against you, your heavenly Father will also forgive you. But if you do not forgive others their sins, your Father will not forgive your sins"* (Matthew 6:14-15, NIV).

Do you see the benefits in letting people off your hook and putting them on God's? In the next chapter, we'll move to Phases 2 and 3.

28

Letting Go of the Hook

I forgive everyone for everything.

You, the Creator of everything, are Sovereign, Providential, and Redemptive.
I am your loved child, redeemed by the blood of Jesus Christ and being transformed daily.
I choose to trust you and your plan before understanding it.
Thank you for your good plan and how you are working it out in my life.
Repenting of all known sin, I choose to live fully forgiven.
I forgive everyone for everything.
I cast every care on you.

"Bear with each other and forgive one another if any of you has a grievance against someone. Forgive as the Lord forgave you" (Colossians 3:13, NIV).

Forgiving everyone of everything is so comprehensive that it sounds extreme. Because it is extreme. You will frequently want to make an exception. Just remember this: every exception is an exception to your health. Unforgiveness is an ongoing cancer that never brings justice but shrivels your soul in bitterness.

Forgiveness basics

God has created you with an innate sense of balance and fairness. When you are in a healthy relationship with another person, your subconscious feeling of balance is so normal as to be taken for granted. All is well.

Have you noticed, however, what happens to a friendship when you loan money to that friend? Provided you did it willingly, there is only a slight upset in the balance of the relationship. You may not even be aware of it at first. But there is a change. One has become a debtor to the other; the equality has been destroyed.

As time goes on, if there is no attempt to repay the debt according to the agreement (or worse yet, the unstated expectation), the relationship begins to become uncomfortable. From there it deteriorates until even close friendships are likely to be destroyed.

The same thing happens when someone offends you. The balance is upset. You have suffered some kind of loss. The loss could be material, as in the case of being cheated or robbed. The loss could also be psychological, as in the loss of dignity or self-esteem if you have been insulted, maligned or betrayed in some way.

This God-given sense of balance tells you that the two sides are no longer matching up as they should. The relationship cannot continue as normal until something is done to even it up again. The human instinct is to inflict an equal injury, to punish the one who is responsible for our loss. That is justice.

The Old Testament remedy sounds fair enough. It was stated this way: "*. . . the punishment must match the injury: a life for a life, an eye for an eye, a tooth for a tooth*" (Exodus 21:23-24, NLT). This is a perfect example of man's need to balance the account. But as the old joke goes, it leads to a lot of blind, toothless people.

Here's a better understanding of how the punishment actually took place. *"If a man hits his male or female slave in the eye and the eye is blinded, he must let the slave go free to compensate for the eye"* (Exodus 21:26, NLT). Fewer blind people this way.

And it comes much closer to Jesus' teaching: *"You have heard the law that says the punishment must match the injury: 'An eye for an eye, and a tooth for a tooth.' But I say, do not resist an evil person! If someone slaps you on the right cheek, offer the other cheek also"* (Matthew 5:38-39, NLT). Although everyone I know has heard that teaching, not many take it seriously, like casting mountains into the sea.

Clearly, God's way of balancing accounts is quite different from ours. He doesn't remove the need for balance: he is, after all, the creator of both order and justice. In Colossians 2:13-14 we see how God restores the balance. *"You were dead because of your sins . . . . Then God made you alive with Christ, for he forgave all our sins.* **He canceled the record of the charges against us and took it away by nailing it to the cross"** (NLT, emphasis added).

The balance must be achieved, but God requires that we achieve it through grace – canceling the charges through the granting of forgiveness.

Phase 2

This is the actual granting of forgiveness. Having battled through the decision that brings you to this point, there is usually no difficulty at this stage UNLESS you attempt to communicate your forgiveness to someone who has not asked for it.

The danger is in your emotional expectations. You naturally feel that your magnanimous gesture should be met with heartfelt thanks and expressions of great remorse from the one who has hurt you. You want affirmation and feelings of warm affection. If that doesn't happen, your emotions are likely to say, "See? I tried to tell you this was a mistake. They're not sorry. They don't even care. Forget this nonsense – it's just making things worse."

Abandoning the process at this point suggests one of two things: either you don't really understand the concept of forgiveness to start with, or you're not emotionally stable enough yet to do the right thing when it's so difficult and counterintuitive.

It's time to remind yourself that your initial decision to forgive was not because they deserved it. Forgiveness is not about the worthiness of the recipient. And neither is your granting of forgiveness dependent on their response. Forgiveness has no such preconditions.

We've learned from experience the danger of *communicating* our decision to forgive when someone has not asked for it. If they have not acknowledged any wrongdoing (whether intentional or not), they will most likely see our forgiveness as a backhanded accusation couched in a display of self-serving pride.

But this is no reason to withhold forgiveness. This is important: Our forgiveness can be complete without the offender ever being aware of either the offense or the forgiveness.

Your choice to forgive someone is unilateral. It does not need their request, permission, or knowledge. This also comes into play when you forgive someone who has already died. You grant forgiveness out of obedience to God. Your relationship with God and your own emotional health are the prime beneficiaries.

Phase 3

The third and final phase of the process is the aftermath. This phase lasts the rest of your life. Though it may be huge from the standpoint of benefits, there is a potential downside that should be minor because it is only a shadow.

Unfortunately, we are sometimes terrorized by shadows, and this one plagues many who complete phases one and two without understanding phase three. The aftermath of forgiveness is totally positive unless you allow this shadow to haunt it.

The shadow is the nagging feeling that you haven't succeeded in your effort to forgive. Something inside keeps saying, "I still have bad feelings whenever I think of that person. I've tried so hard but I guess I'm just not capable of doing it. Why can't I forgive? I feel so guilty when I think about it."

This shadow is both pervasive and crippling. You can beat yourself up and feel like a failure if you haven't distinguished fact from feeling.

Forgiveness is a judicial transaction. If you have granted it, the deed is done. It is now historical fact. Your feelings may take a long time to catch up, but that doesn't change the fact. Only when you focus on your feelings do you have cause to doubt the fact.

These following illustrations are quite common and simplistic, but they should help you apply the truth to an area that may still seem fuzzy.

Graduation day

Do you remember when you graduated from high school? It came as no surprise. You had grown and worked for seventeen or eighteen years in preparation for this major event.

Chances are pretty good that much of your senior year felt like marking time until you would finally be done with this chapter of your development and be able to move into adult life.

Do you remember reaching out and receiving your diploma? There were probably some strange emotions that day: the bittersweet excitement of new horizons mixed with the parting of old friends and the knowledge that your world was about to change radically and would never be the same again.

Of all the things you thought and felt, there is one I can almost guarantee you did not feel. You didn't *feel* graduated.

Wedding day

Or how about the day of your wedding? You had spent months planning the event. You may have been fortunate enough to receive some valuable premarital counseling.

Certainly you spent a lot of time daydreaming about what marriage would be like with that perfect person you had found.

Suddenly the ceremony, which seemed like a surreal dream, was concluding and from somewhere in the distance you heard the words, "I now pronounce you man and wife."

But unless you're quite an exception, you didn't *feel* any different. You didn't *feel* married.

Had you signed the certificate? Had you said, "I do"? Were you legally married? Of course. So, which was more accurate, the fact or your feelings?

Three basic principles

1. There is often a discrepancy between fact and feeling. This is obvious.

2. This discrepancy is uncomfortable because it upsets your sense of balance. Your self-dialogue routinely creates a story to make sense of discrepancies, a story that protects your self-image. This puts the feelings at the forefront and blurs the facts to fit accordingly. It satisfies you, although it may not totally agree with anyone else's account of what happened.

If, on the other hand, you focus on the facts, over time your feelings will conform to the facts. The "fact" we're talking about at the moment is that you made a deliberate choice to forgive. Don't let your feelings blur the fact; allow them time to align to it.

As important as it is to understand these first two principles, they are relatively useless without the third one.

3. You can choose your own focus. One of the greatest powers God has bestowed upon you as a human being is the power to choose your focus. While there is much of existentialist philosophy that is questionable, Kierkegaard correctly asserted that you are not a pawn to either your genetic makeup or your environment. You have the ability, unique in all of creation, to escape those confines and alter the reality they would otherwise dictate.

The concept of self-consciousness has long been accepted by science as one of the most distinguishing features separating humanity from the rest of the animal kingdom. You are aware of your uniqueness as an individual, distinct from all other objects and beings. You can think in the abstract, mentally picturing yourself and imagining various scenarios. This ability empowers you to live above the realm of instinct and to exert an influence on reality that is truly creative. This is a small part of what it means to be created *"in the image of God"* (Genesis 1:27, ESV).

Applying all of this to forgiveness

Forgiveness is both a judicial and an accounting term. In the halls of justice, it is dropping the charges or granting a pardon. In accounting, it is writing off a debt, declaring it no longer due – whether it has been repaid or not.

Don't be confused by misconceptions of what forgiveness is and is not. Forgiveness is not a feeling. It is not denial. It is not justifying. It is not excusing. It is not just asking God to do it. It is not forgetting. It is not trusting. It is not reconciliation. It is not compatibility. It is not earned. It is not optional.

It is simply an evening of the accounts through your deliberate decision to extend grace as God has extended it to you. It is wiping out the debt, not through repayment, but through forgiving it.

Forgiveness is saying, "I no longer hold this hurt against you, and I relinquish any and all attempts to make it right by getting even. I cancel the debt. You don't owe me any longer." Here it is in a single sentence. Forgiveness is removing an offense from the offender's page in your ledger of accounts.

And you've done this. You've chosen to remove the offense from your ledger, giving up your "right" to restore balance through some other means.

Don't let your feelings – which may take longer to heal – rob you of your freedom. Although you can never earn forgiveness, you can earn freedom by granting forgiveness to others.

Thank God and rejoice in your freedom. And now that you've done the hard work of emptying your hook, dream a little about how you might work toward letting go of the hook itself.

You're on the home stretch!

You've nearly completed the reading. I pray that you are already experiencing renewed hope, deeper trust, and consistent gratitude – all components of enduring peace.

A lot is riding on the new habits you develop. As the Peace Credo becomes a regular feature of your day, it transforms your perspective (what you see), your thinking (how you process what you see) and your decisions (the actions that represent you to the outside world).

If this book is helping you, would you consider doing me a huge favor? I'd love to hear from you. It would also be a great benefit to me if you would take a few minutes to leave a book review on Amazon. Please see the simple instructions at the end of the "About the Author" section. Thank you and God bless.

29

The Final Line

I cast every care on you.

> You, the Creator of everything, are Sovereign, Providential, and Redemptive.
> I am your loved child, redeemed by the blood of Jesus Christ and being transformed daily.
> I choose to trust you and your plan before understanding it.
> Thank you for your good plan and how you are working it out in my life.
> Repenting of all known sin, I choose to live fully forgiven.
> I forgive everyone for everything.
> **I cast every care on you.**

I cast every care on you. This final line in the Peace Credo couldn't be simpler – in theory. But in practice, it is anything but natural.

What are your cares?
To catch a glimpse of what this chapter can do for you, take a moment to list your top three cares. Are you concerned about your finances? Most people are. How about your health? Your spouse? Your kids and grandkids? Your coworkers? Your boss? Problems at church? At school?

Don't limit this to just fears and worries. Anything you care about is a care, including hopes, dreams, and aspirations. If your heart is set on something, God cares about it as well for two reasons: first, he wants to bless you because you are his loved child. Second, he wants to protect you from allowing something to capture your heart to the point of becoming an obsession, an idol, that would end in disappointment. *"Above all else, **guard your affections**. For they influence **everything else** in your life"* (Proverbs 4:23, TLB, emphasis added).

Casting hopes, dreams, and aspirations on God does not mean throwing them away. Here's the basic principle: *"In everything you do, put God first, and he will direct you and crown your efforts with success"* (Proverbs 3:6, TLB).

Why your list is important – recognizing means and ends

After you've made an initial list of cares and thought for a moment about their importance to you, consider this question: What would you give to ensure them – so that the things you most fear would not come to pass and the things you most desire would be granted?

Would you give up peace and happiness for them? I doubt it. You would probably say that the reason you care about them in the first place is because you think avoiding the bad ones and getting the good ones is what will lead to peace and happiness.

To help put things in perspective, determine which cares in your list are means and which are ends. This is not difficult. The difficult part is determining whether any given set of means can guarantee the desired ends.

Can you be rich and miserable? Many people are. Can you be healthy and miserable? Ditto. Can you be famous, successful in your career, extremely talented, etc., and be miserable? Double Ditto. No one wants to pursue all the means they think will lead to peace and happiness only to find emptiness and disappointment. There's a better way. Wouldn't you rather be like Paul, able to say that you have learned the *"secret of contentment"* (TLB), the *"recipe for being happy"* (MSG) in *"any and every circumstance"* (NASB)?

This worked for Paul all the time, even when he was in prison. *"I've learned by now to be quite content whatever my circumstances. I'm just as happy with little as with much, with much as with little. I've found the recipe for being happy whether full or hungry, hands full or hands empty. Whatever I have, wherever I am, I can make it through anything in the One who makes me who I am"* (Philippians 4:12-13, MSG).

This means-and-ends discussion is intended to help you avoid one thing while encouraging you toward another. Avoid putting too much confidence in the means. Instead, hold them loosely while confidently and joyfully casting them on your loving Father.

Why should you "cast every care" on God?

1 Peter 5:7 is the source for this final line in the Peace Credo. Consider these various translations of the verse. What reason do they all point to for casting your cares on God?

> *"Cast all your care upon Him, because He cares for you"* (MEV).

> *"You can throw the whole weight of your anxieties upon him, for you are his personal concern"*
> (PHILLIPS).

> *"Let him have all your worries and cares, for he is always thinking about you and watching everything that concerns you"* (TLB).

> *"Give all your worries and cares to God, for he cares about you"* (NLT).

> *"Live carefree before God; he is most careful with you"* (MSG).

> *"Pour out all your worries and stress upon him and leave them there, for he always tenderly cares for you"* (TPT).

The obvious answer is that God cares deeply about you. And notice that most of these verses use the word "all" to emphasize the cares you should cast. God is offering to engage with you in the totality of your concerns, not just the religious stuff.

The Peace Credo uses the words "every care" to emphasize that each care occupies its own place of importance in your life. Each one is uniquely qualified to benefit from your Father's providential oversight and intervention.

In further answer to the question of why you should cast every care on God, realize that everything in the Peace Credo has built to this last line. Every preceding line contributes to the solid foundation for confidently casting your cares on God.

God's identity: *You, the Creator of everything, are Sovereign, Providential, and Redemptive.* To what higher authority could you go for help?

Your identity: *I am your loved child, redeemed by the blood of Jesus Christ and being transformed daily.* Who could care more about your welfare?

Trusting: *I choose to trust you and your plan before understanding it.* Because of who God is and who you are.

Grateful: *Thank you for your good plan and how you are working it out in my life.* God alone can guarantee the successful conclusion of his plan as he *"works all things together for good."*

Forgiven: *Repenting of all known sin, I choose to live fully forgiven.* Guilt and shame no longer separate you from full access to God's care and blessing.

Relationally free: *I forgive everyone for everything.* You are under bondage to no one.

Free at last and ready to cast

You are now perfectly positioned to cast your cares and experience the inner peace God has for you.

Casting strategies

Let's use a fishing metaphor to illustrate a few problems you might encounter in your attempt to cast every care on God. You are casting bait (cares) with the hope of getting something better.

Pretend casting

Everything is set: the weights, bobber, hook, and bait – all ready to be cast. You go into your backswing and then whip the rod forward with what looks like good aim. But you never release the line. You're just going through the motions with no intention of fishing. Don't know who you're trying to please, but it's all for show. Great way to keep the bait.

Casting and retrieving
This time you release the line and make a great cast. But you have no patience because you have no confidence. You immediately reel the line back in so you can remain in control. Another good way to keep the bait, but that's not the goal.

Casting and waiting
This one is not a problem; it's the way to go. You've done your part – all the appropriate prep. You cast, release, and wait patiently for God to do his part. You're open to his direction regarding any adjustments you should make. You realize how blessed you are to have God as your partner.

Casting and forgetting
This one goes to the opposite extreme of the first two. There may be times when something like this is appropriate – perhaps with some past hurts. Or with problems so far beyond your circle of responsibility or influence that all you can do is pray and release them, trusting God to do what only he can do. But in areas where you retain some responsibility or influence, casting and waiting is better.

Casting and leaving
Most of our cares call for some degree of responsibility from us. We don't just cast the line and walk away

never to return, but there is one major exception. We don't want the bait back. Worry, fear, anxiety, stress, obsession – we cast all these stinky bits of garbage with no desire to take them back home with us.

What does your casting look like? If you find yourself reeling the bait back in – whether it's a day, an hour, or a minute later – cast it again. God will faithfully do his part in taking it from you, but your part in leaving it with him is a war with the enemy.

The last thing Satan wants is your freedom. You can win battles, but the war isn't won without repetition.

This is why the Peace Credo exists:

- To routinely replace Satan's deceptions with God's truth (ultimate reality).
- To get the truth from your head to your heart.
- To train your intuition to see, interpret, and respond with wisdom.
- To create positive habits that yield inner peace.

Memorize it. Use it to further build your biblical worldview. Meditate on the underlying Scriptures as you give thanks and cast your cares.

Closing reminder

Do you remember what started this whole journey for me five years ago? The realization that I had two huge needs – needs that were foundational to everything else in my life. First, to grow in my awareness of God's presence. Second, to grow in my trust in him and how he is working out his plan in my life.

Awareness and trust.

Simple.

Profound.

Life changers.

They open the door to the Master Craftsman.

The Peace Credo has been instrumental in raising both my awareness and my trust as it wears a deep path in my head and heart. Over and over I choose to trust, whether I understand a lot or nothing, because the One I trust has proven himself to be trustworthy.

When all else fails – and most of it will – he remains my loving Father who just happens to be Sovereign, Providential, and Redemptive.

Paul's instruction to the Philippians two thousand years ago has never been timelier. It is exactly what we need today. *"Don't worry about anything; instead, pray about everything. Tell God what you need, and thank him for all he has done. Then you will experience* **God's peace,** *which exceeds anything we can understand.* **His peace** *will guard your hearts and minds as you live in Christ Jesus"* (Philippians 4:6-7, NLT, emphasis added).

Steve and Maria Gardner

Steve is an author, editor, and songwriter. He has written and edited books, multi-media products, and global training materials for Crown Financial Ministries, Compass – finances God's Way, Emerging Young Leaders, Ken Blanchard's Lead Like Jesus, *Pilgrim's Progress—Journey to Heaven* (the movie), the Southern Baptist Convention, the American Bible Society.

After graduating from Wheaton College in 1971 with a B.A. in Anthropology, Steve and his wife, Maria, traveled five continents as full-time concert and recording artists until 1996. They recorded 16 albums of largely original music while performing more than 4,000 concerts and 1,000 TV appearances. They hosted "Words of Hope," a weekly TV show, and "Marriage Matters," a monthly radio program. Steve also hosted "Three Men and a Book," a monthly live radio program.

Married for more than 53 years, Steve and Maria have one daughter and three grandchildren. Steve enjoys a variety of sports including tennis, squash, racquetball, pickleball, scuba, and downhill skiing.

Steve's mission: To aggressively pursue God's leading in every area of my life so that I can influence others by word and example to be followers of Christ.

If **40 Seconds to Inner Peace** has been helpful to you, it will likely help your family and friends as well. Please share it with them by posting on Facebook and any other social platforms you use.

Your feedback and support in a review on Amazon would also help us expand our outreach. Just go to the listing and click on the Customer Reviews. Right under the star bars on the left side is an opportunity to "Review this product."

Thank you, and peace to your house.

www.ingramcontent.com/pod-product-compliance
Lightning Source LLC
Chambersburg PA
CBHW051828160426
43209CB00040B/1980/J